Data Exploration Using Example-Based Methods

Synthesis Lectures on Data Management

Editor
H.V. Jagadish, *University of Michigan*

Founding Editor
M. Tamer Özsu, *University of Waterloo*

Synthesis Lectures on Data Management is edited by H.V. Jagadish of the University of Michigan. The series publishes 80–150 page publications on topics pertaining to data management. Topics include query languages, database system architectures, transaction management, data warehousing, XML and databases, data stream systems, wide scale data distribution, multimedia data management, data mining, and related subjects.

Data Exploration Using Example-Based Methods
Matteo Lissandrini, Davide Mottin, Themis Palpanas, and Yannis Velegrakis
2018

Querying Graphs
Angela Bonifati, George Fletcher, Hannes Voigt, and Nikolay Yakovets
2018

Query Processing over Incomplete Databases
Yunjun Gao and Xiaoye Miao
2018

Natural Language Data Management and Interfaces
Yunyao Li and Davood Rafiei
2018

Human Interaction with Graphs: A Visual Querying Perspective
Sourav S. Bhowmick, Byron Choi, and Chengkai Li
2018

On Uncertain Graphs
Arijit Khan, Yuan Ye, and Lei Chen
2018

Data Processing on FPGAs
Jens Teubner and Louis Woods
2013

Perspectives on Business Intelligence
Raymond T. Ng, Patricia C. Arocena, Denilson Barbosa, Giuseppe Carenini, Luiz Gomes, Jr.,
Stephan Jou, Rock Anthony Leung, Evangelos Milios, Renée J. Miller, John Mylopoulos, Rachel
A. Pottinger, Frank Tompa, and Eric Yu
2013

Semantics Empowered Web 3.0: Managing Enterprise, Social, Sensor, and Cloud-based
Data and Services for Advanced Applications
Amit Sheth and Krishnaprasad Thirunarayan
2012

Data Management in the Cloud: Challenges and Opportunities
Divyakant Agrawal, Sudipto Das, and Amr El Abbadi
2012

Query Processing over Uncertain Databases
Lei Chen and Xiang Lian
2012

Foundations of Data Quality Management
Wenfei Fan and Floris Geerts
2012

Incomplete Data and Data Dependencies in Relational Databases
Sergio Greco, Cristian Molinaro, and Francesca Spezzano
2012

Business Processes: A Database Perspective
Daniel Deutch and Tova Milo
2012

Data Protection from Insider Threats
Elisa Bertino
2012

Deep Web Query Interface Understanding and Integration
Eduard C. Dragut, Weiyi Meng, and Clement T. Yu
2012

P2P Techniques for Decentralized Applications
Esther Pacitti, Reza Akbarinia, and Manal El-Dick
2012

Data Exploration Using Example-Based Methods

Matteo Lissandrini, Davide Mottin, Themis Palpanas, and Yannis Velegrakis

ISBN: 978-3-031-00738-5   paperback
ISBN: 978-3-031-01866-4   ebook
ISBN: 978-3-031-00093-5   hardcover

DOI 10.1007/978-3-031-01866-4

A Publication in the Springer series
SYNTHESIS LECTURES ON DATA MANAGEMENT

Lecture #53
Series Editor: H.V. Jagadish, *University of Michigan*
Founding Editor: M. Tamer Özsu, *University of Waterloo*
Series ISSN
Print 2153-5418   Electronic 2153-5426

Data Exploration Using Example-Based Methods

Matteo Lissandrini
Aalborg University

Davide Mottin
Aarhus University

Themis Palpanas
Paris Descartes University

Yannis Velegrakis
University of Trento

SYNTHESIS LECTURES ON DATA MANAGEMENT #53

ABSTRACT

Data usually comes in a plethora of formats and dimensions, rendering the exploration and information extraction processes challenging. Thus, being able to perform exploratory analyses in the data with the intent of having an immediate glimpse on some of the data properties is becoming crucial. Exploratory analyses should be simple enough to avoid complicate declarative languages (such as SQL) and mechanisms, and at the same time retain the flexibility and expressiveness of such languages. Recently, we have witnessed a rediscovery of the so-called *example-based methods*, in which the user, or the analyst, circumvents query languages by using examples as input. An example is a representative of the intended results, or in other words, an item from the result set. Example-based methods exploit inherent characteristics of the data to infer the results that the user has in mind, but may not able to (easily) express. They can be useful in cases where a user is looking for information in an unfamiliar dataset, when the task is particularly challenging like finding duplicate items, or simply when they are exploring the data. In this book, we present an excursus over the main methods for exploratory analysis, with a particular focus on example-based methods. We show how that different data types require different techniques, and present algorithms that are specifically designed for relational, textual, and graph data. The book presents also the challenges and the new frontiers of machine learning in online settings which recently attracted the attention of the database community. The lecture concludes with a vision for further research and applications in this area.

KEYWORDS

search by example, data exploration, information retrieval, data management

Contents

Preface

Exploration is one of the primordial ways to accrue knowledge about the world and its nature. It describes the act of becoming familiar with something by testing or experimenting, and at the same time it evokes the image of a traveler traversing a new territory. As we accumulate, mostly automatically, data at unprecedented volumes and speed, our datasets have become less and less familiar to us. In this context we speak of **exploratory search** as of the process of gradual discovery and understanding of the portion of the data that is pertinent to an often-times vague user's information need. Contrary to traditional search, where the desired result is well defined and the focus is on precision and performance, exploratory search usually starts from a *tentative query* that hopefully leads to answers at least partially relevant and that can provide cues about the next query. By understanding the distinction between a traditional query and an exploratory query, we can change the semantics of the user input: instead of a strict prescription of the contents of the result-set, we provide a hint of what is relevant. This shift in semantics has led to a number of methods having in common the very specific paradigm of *search by-example*. Search by-example receives as query a set of example members of the answer set. The search system then infers the entire answer set based on the given examples and any additional information provided by the underlying database.

With this book we have surveyed more than 200 research sources to highlight the main example-based techniques for relational, graph, and textual data. The book provides insights on how these example-based search systems can be employed by expert and non-expert users in retrieving the portion of the data that is relevant to their interest, while avoiding the use of complex query languages. We hope this book answers the questions and builds the necessary knowledge to those interested in constructing new data exploration systems.

Graduate students would hopefully deepen their interest in the subject and being involved in the new challenges and opportunities allowed by the powerful exploration method of search-by-example. Researchers and practitioners working in the area will probably find new insights for further improving their approaches and systems.

Matteo Lissandrini, Davide Mottin, Themis Palpanas, and Yannis Velegrakis
July 2018

Acknowledgments

We would like to sincerely thank the authors of the referenced papers for providing us with extra support material that greatly helped the writing of this book, as well as the reviewers for their detailed and constructive comments.

Matteo Lissandrini, Davide Mottin, Themis Palpanas, and Yannis Velegrakis
July 2018

CHAPTER 1

Introduction

Example is always more efficacious than precept.

—Samuel Johnson
"The History of Rasselas, Prince of Abissinia" (1759, Chapter 29)

In today's world, we produce data at an unprecedented pace. Such data is created by social networks, personal devices, and home applications, as well as by companies, scientific laboratories, and the public sector. The heterogeneous and rapidly changing nature of those datasets, alongside the need to integrate them with evolving information needs, invalidates a common assumption on which data analysis usually relies: that the data analyst is a *"data expert."* That is, a person fully aware of the information contained in the dataset, and able to directly distill the desired knowledge (with the appropriate tools). In this context, *queries* play an essential role, since they allow analysts to specify the pieces of information of interest.

Data management systems usually assume user expertise in formulating precise questions to retrieve the desired information or reckon a broad knowledge of the data. Hence, such systems often require an initial, *Data Exploration* phase [Idreos et al., 2007], where the user familiarizes themselves with the data and the system. During this exploratory phase, users acquire the necessary information about the data and their structure and identify queries to retrieve the desired information.

Data exploration includes methods to efficiently extract knowledge from data, even if we do not know what exactly we are looking for, nor how to precisely describe our needs [Idreos et al., 2015]. In such exploration, the user progressively acquires the knowledge by issuing a sequence of generic queries to gather intelligence about the data. Therefore, efficiency is a keystone in data exploration systems that require to process a large number of queries. The system may (quickly) provide approximate summaries of the characteristics of the data to support such queries.

Example 1.1   Jodi is a sales manager for Brand X, which sells products to companies. Brand X is expanding in a new region and has recently acquired a database of the companies located there. *Jodi has access to this database, and now is looking for companies to contact as new possible customers.* Naturally, not all of the companies match the ideal type of customers for Brand X's products.

Jodi does not know the content of the database but remembers some basics of SQL and writes a first *exploratory* query: `SELECT * FROM TABLE ` `` `Companies'. ``

A quick look to the results provides a preliminary understanding of the companies in the database and some of their characteristics. Which of these companies operate in an industry that can make use of Brand X products? Which of those are large enough to afford Brand X premium service, but not so large to have that in-house already? Naturally, the desired customers would be buried among the results of the above query, which unfortunately are too many to be of practical use. How can Jodi retrieve the companies that match their interest?

Several techniques have been recently developed to help users find their way through large and unfamiliar datasets and toward the desired information. Visual data exploration techniques [Parameswaran et al., 2013, Vartak et al., 2017, Wu et al., 2014] provide new tools and new exploration interfaces that offer intuitive visualizations of datasets and answer-sets. These systems work hand-in-hand with query recommendations techniques. For instance, Chatzopoulou et al. [2009] and Sadikov et al. [2010] try to discover the query intent by analyzing previous similar queries, and then suggest queries with the same or analogous intent.

As mentioned earlier, given the vagueness of such exploratory tasks, many queries are submitted by the user in rapid succession, and the system needs to answer several exploratory queries very quickly. To this end, Hellerstein et al. [1997] and Kersten et al. [2011] propose optimizations for online and approximate query processing to provide quick, approximate answers to exploratory queries. Moreover, Khoussainova et al. [2009] studied collaborative databases, where users can share findings and queries as well, and Cherniack et al. [2001] employed user profiles to understand the user preference and intent better.

Therefore, we see how essential directions for data exploration include user interfaces for query result visualization, and middleware for efficient data prefetching, query approximation, adaptive indexing, and storage. Even though these directions address users with knowledge about the domain, the system, and the analysis tool, they do require additional effort from novice users, since a critical requirement is still the domain knowledge and expert use of queries.

1.1   EXAMPLE-DRIVEN EXPLORATION

Data exploration describes the initial phase in which the user is *trying to understand* if the data at hand contains any relevant information and in what form. However, this phase still relies on the user ability to formulate some *search queries*, even if they are vague or imprecise. As richer information sources become available to the broad public, accessing and understanding such data attracts an increasingly larger population of non-expert users that desire to analyze the data. Several techniques assist users in this exploratory search process (e.g., consider the smart home assistants, such as Alexa, Siri, and Google Home) which, nevertheless, require users to formulate rather specific and precise queries.

Example 1.2   A frequent traveler has just visited Berlin and was fascinated by the vibrant life of the city. They would like to ask to their home assistant "Is there any other city like Berlin?" However, the answer provided by the home assistant is probably disappointing and most probably concerning only Berlin itself. To get the expected answer, they need to ask a precise question, such as "Find all the big European cities with vibrant music and art scene."

Such possible scenario highlights the struggle of the user toward traditional search systems, which often require very well defined search terms. Even so, the latter question can be hardly answered, given the different aspects (music, art, big city, Europe) implied by request. Existing search systems indeed provide powerful and expressive query mechanisms, which allow answering complex questions very quickly, but require expertise in search languages and a clear idea of the required information. These information search systems usually rely on "query lookup" paradigms employing query-matching problems where the query contains the conditions that describe a clear information need, and answers are all those items that match the query conditions. Hence, a user with unclear ideas and insufficient knowledge of the system and the data, demands completely different tools that can help them in *interpreting the data*, *identifying the characteristics* of the desired answer, and finally, *retrieving such answer efficiently*.

Exploratory search, as described by White and Roth [2009], has proposed a remedy for the rigidity of existing search systems. By offering an alternative to the query-lookup paradigm of search systems, exploratory search guides the user toward the answer, even if the description of such an answer is unclear or ill-defined. Exploratory search constitutes the search for the right data, information, and query. The existing body of work assumes the user is willing to refine the search to gather the required information progressively. This assumption still requires that users have a minimum level of expertise in the search method. Some works [Cetintemel et al., 2013, Chatzopoulou et al., 2009, Kersten et al., 2011] acknowledged that it is often hard for a user to write the right query. Their solution is a search system that understands the user's intent and offers the guidance to refine the query, if necessary. Such systems often overload the user with an unnecessarily large number of requests and refinements. Moreover, they cannot be of help to all those users that are not able to formulate any query at all.

In this book, we survey *example-based* methods that take an entirely different perspective to data exploration: *the user can express a query through a part of the answer, that is, with an example.* The primary intuition is that users can better express themselves through some examples of an object, a situation, an event, or document that are familiar to them instead of an elaborate description of the answers. To illustrate this intuition we borrow an excerpt from Wille [2009]:

> … in many situations one has only a vague knowledge of a context although many of its concepts are fairly clear. For instance, it seems to be impossible to write down a comprehensive context of musical instruments, but everyone uses concepts as violin,

trumpet, guitar, string instrument, etc. and meaningful sentences such as "a violin is
a string instrument."

—Wille [2009]

Example-based methods come to play in all those cases in which the user is aware of some items
that match (at least partially) their interest. A sales manager that tries to identify new customers
in a database of companies, a lawyer trying to find similar cases to the one they are defending,
a researcher trying to find papers related to the topic of their study, or a tourist that is planning
a new trip, those are all cases in which it is easier to use examples than trying to describe the
intention with a query.

Existing by-example methods are used to infer SQL queries from some example tuples,
identify rules to align two databases, and find distinct entities that represent the same object. For
documents, example-based methods identify the topics of interest from the example to return
other unexpected documents. In a graph, starting from a structure, they navigate the nodes and
edges conveniently and show relevant areas and similar objects or structures. In this book, we
provide an extensive compendium of such example-based methods, as well as insights on how
to embed them in exploratory search systems.

Example 1.3   Consider the example of the customer database again. Jodi is looking for new
companies to expand Brand X customer base. To identify candidate customers, Jodi can look
at the characteristics of their current customers (industry sector, net-worth, revenue) and then
concoct some filters to the query to retrieve *companies similar to the current customers*. Wouldn't
it be simpler for Jodi to present to the database some tuples describing their current customers,
and let the system identify the similar ones?

Example-based search is one of the most recent additions to the backpack of the data-
explorer. A tool that, contrary to all the previous ones, **removes the need for the user to specify
a query**. They allow exploration in a bottom-up approach, that is, by starting from instances of
interest they enable the user to identify general relationships and characteristics that characterize
both the known examples and also other, unknown, instances. Moreover, example-based methods can expand the capabilities of existing exploration system. For example, classical exploration
methods can help users discover relevant portions or items with some statistically significant
characteristics, and, then, the user can start to investigate such situations by giving examples
based on these data-points.

The research community has resorted to the use of *examples* as an ideal proxy for exploratory queries. One of the earliest attempts to bring examples as a query method is called
query-by-example (QBE) and was studied by Zloof [1975]. The main idea was to help the user
in the query formulation, allowing them to specify the shape of the results in terms of templates
for tuples, i.e., examples. Query-by-example has been lately revisited, and the use of examples
have found application in several areas across various data types. The definition of an example
has transformed from a mere template to the representative of the intended results the user

would like to have. These example-based approaches are then fundamentally different from the initial query-by-example idea.

1.1.1 PROBLEM FORMULATION

To formalize this new paradigm, we introduce a more general definition of example-based queries, where we are querying the data through examples. *An example-based query is a subset of elements of the desired result-set that identifies the query itself.* The system then has to retrieve the remaining members of the (full) answer-set to which the examples belong.

Assume a universe of candidate objects $\mathcal{U}$ (e.g., tuples, entities, documents, graph nodes or structures), among which we identify a subset of relevant elements or instances ($\mathcal{A} \subseteq \mathcal{U}$) that the user is trying to retrieve; these are the desired answers. Assume also that the user is aware of only a subset of the instances, for which they know to be part of the desired answers; these are *examples* of the desired answers ($\mathcal{E} \subset \mathcal{A}$). Then, there exists a set of characteristics (or specifications) that describes all members of $\mathcal{A}$. In other words, we consider the existence of a query Q that depends on the data model, such that the set $\mathcal{A}$ is the set of answers obtained by applying Q over $\mathcal{U}$ ($\mathcal{A} = Q(\mathcal{U})$). Yet, the user only knows the subset $\mathcal{E}$, and is not aware of Q: the goal is to identify the entire set $\mathcal{A}$ starting from $\mathcal{E}$. Therefore, the example-based query paradigm is defined as follows.

Problem 1.4 Example-based query paradigm

Given a universe $\mathcal{U}$ of objects, an unknown set of desired answers $\mathcal{A} \subset \mathcal{U}$, and a known set of examples $\mathcal{E} \subseteq \mathcal{A}$, **find** a query Q, such that $\mathcal{E} \subseteq Q(\mathcal{U}) = \mathcal{A}$.

This paradigm enables exploration in a new way: instead of trying to summarize the general characteristics of a large dataset, move in the opposite direction: start from a small set of known answers to arrive to a broader set of desired results. We note that the query Q can be the actual object of the search (as it distills the set of characteristics that the desired answers should satisfy), or it can just be a partial specification that exploits similarities to the examples $\mathcal{E}$. Observe also that the paradigm is general, in the sense that the nature of the elements and the query can be arbitrarily rich: as we will see, a single example may be an entire set of objects from the dataset, so that the set E is a set of sets. The query Q should then define which objects form a valid set.

1.1.2 APPLICATIONS OF EXAMPLE-BASED METHODS

The by-example query paradigm has been successfully applied to relational, graph, and textual data. We note that the flexibility of using examples as queries does not compromise the richness of the results, yet, it overcomes the ambiguity of simple keyword search, that is the first-class-citizen in information retrieval as a more user-friendly search paradigm.

On the other hand, as presented by Idreos et al. [2015], while data exploration techniques assume the user is willing to pose several exploratory queries, the use of examples requires almost no supervision from the user perspective, making example-based methods a more palatable choice for novice users, as well as for practitioners. This new functionality can empower existing data exploration methods with a complementary tool: whenever a query is too complicated to be expressed with a query language, such as SQL, examples represent a natural alternative. When the goal is to probe the database and expand the search around a small set of relevant data-points, example-based query paradigms are the most appropriate tools for the job.

Example-based exploration is a middle ground between the user interface, and the middleware/hardware, enabling new functionalities for the former and allowing more natural exploitation of the latter. We present this extended stack in Figure 1.1. The by-example search paradigm provides an additional layer, which bridges the gap between natural and interpretable data access and powerful search systems. We note that this paradigm can, in principle, handle multiple data-models, although this possibility is not fully explored yet. Moreover, example-based approaches invite contributions from the machine learning area, useful for understanding the vague user needs, as well as for enriching user interfaces and middleware techniques.

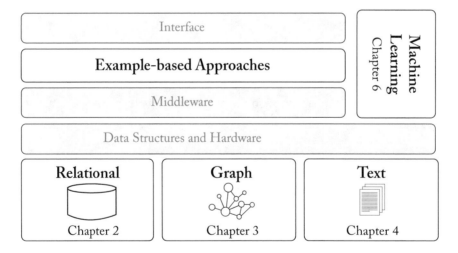

Figure 1.1: Data-Exploration with example-based techniques covered in this book. Techniques for Relational Data are presented in Chapter 2, for Graph Data are presented in Chapter 3, and for Text in Chapter 4. We also present Machine Learning methods in Chapter 6.

1.2   ROAD MAP

In this book, we aim at describing the main developments of example-based query paradigms as a powerful and robust method for exploratory data analysis.

Part I of the book discusses the current main techniques for relational, textual, and graph data. For each data-model, a dedicated section contrasts the needs of exploratory search to the hardness of the existing query languages and advocates the need for different query methods. We introduce the example-based methods as flexible delegates for more complex queries that would otherwise need to be expressed through a traditional query that is either very complex or too vague. We discuss cases where queries cannot be adequately expressed in declarative languages because of information needs that are hard to communicate.

In this part of the book, for the three key data-models, we present the algorithms for example-driven exploration (and related tasks), show how they work, and demonstrate their ability to (conceptually) infer very complex queries from simple examples. We also highlight the differences among different query intents, and how they translate for the different data-types. We also focus on the scalability perspective, presenting the most critical intuitions, data-structures, and theoretical guarantees that allow the presented methods to be employed in large and high-dimensional datasets.

Part II of the book focuses on the latest developments of machine learning and how they can be employed to discover user intentions in an online fashion progressively. We introduce some old methods based on relevance feedback and show some recent applications that include active learning and active search.

The last chapter of the book is dedicated to the challenges and open research questions. Exploratory search based on examples is rapidly attracting attention and getting traction, however, the support for such techniques in modern data management systems is lagging. Some challenges have already been discussed in recent vision papers, such as Wasay et al. [2015] and Wu et al. [2014]. We also discuss the significant challenges that are related to this vision, and how an example-based query paradigm could fit into the future exploratory search system.

PART I

Example-Based Approaches

CHAPTER 2

Relational Data

One look at relational data and the scenario resembles those offices with vast piles of documents organized in archives. The documents in our analogy illustrate the tuples and the archives the tables in a relational database. Relational databases superseded paper archives allowing the convenient categorization of a significant amount of information. The exploration of such databases relies on declarative languages, such as SQL [Codd, 1970], which appear complicated at the eyes of non-expert users.

In the relational world, a database can represent a shoe store, the shoes the single items or tuples in the database, while a user's desired shoes is a tacit SQL query on such database. A question emerges: could the database be smart enough to recognize which shoes the customer wants without the need to specify all the detailed characteristics? Example-based approaches are an expressive mean to solve complex tasks, such as recovering an implicit user query, guiding users toward answers of interest, and inferring mapping-rules between database schemas.

Example 2.1 Consider the case of a sales manager, Jodi, working for Brand X. Brand X intends to automatize the process of finding high-quality customers, employees, and collaborators. Defining complex queries for such tasks requires thorough database expertise. Moreover, each time new datasets are added in the database of Brand X, the queries need to be adapted. The questions Jodi needs to answer are: How can I formulate complex queries knowing only a few names of past customers (e.g., how can I find other companies selling similar products) (Section 2.2)? How can I import and integrate a new dataset of potential customers (Section 2.3)? How can I remove duplicates and errors from our database (Section 2.4)?

Such approaches reminisce *provenance and data lineage* [Buneman et al., 2004, De, 2012] (Herschel et al. [2017] published a recent survey on provenance). Provenance keeps track of and tries to reconstruct the query that generates a table, a view, or a set of results. To some extent, provenance is an example-based approach in which the user has to provide the complete result of a query as input. Despite the similarity between the two tasks, we note that provenance entails an exhaustive description of the result for analytics purpose, while users often provide incomplete and inaccurate specifications.

Another line of research focuses on *why-not queries* [Tran and Chan, 2010] which takes as input a query whose result is missing some item, and the task is to understand and provide explanations about the missing item. Why-not queries are useful analysis instruments in which examples help to reformulate the current query to obtain the desired result set. It follows that why-not queries also relate to *query refinement* [Mottin et al., 2013] and *reformulation* [Chaudhuri, 1990]. However, the aforementioned problems require a fully specified, albeit imprecise, query from the user which is usually not provided in the cases we study.

Exploring Relations: The relational model is a flexible representation for structured data with a predefined structure. Yet, its flexibility comes to the price of intuitiveness for the user. Its principal declarative query language, SQL, is not within just anyone's reach and requires expertise and understanding of the underlying model.

Data exploration of relational datasets is a vital paradigm to retrieve information when we are not sure of what we are looking for [Idreos et al., 2015]. Such tools significantly improve the usability of systems and adaptivity toward new queries [Idreos et al., 2007], and adapt to vague information needs. On a similar vein, examples provide an intelligible manner for describing complex tasks without the aid of complex declarative query languages. Complex tasks, such as query formulation, schema mapping, and entity matching become suddenly intuitive and pleasant.

Exploration methods for relational data start from tuples, tuple pairs, or example datasets to perform the task above in a more instinctive and comprehensible fashion.

This chapter introduces example-based approaches for relational data, with an intended focus on *reverse engineering queries* (Section 2.2), which aids the user in query formulation. Section 2.3 turns the attention to *schema mapping*, a specialized and complex task which requires usually specific skills and tools, such as Clio [Fagin et al., 2009]. We also analyze *entity matching*, traditionally performed with learning approaches or handcrafted rules, which has recently resorted to example-based solutions (Section 2.4). Finally, we present a selection of *example-based systems* that proposes interfaces for example-based methods through query reformulation and tree-like navigation (Section 2.5).

2.1   PRELIMINARIES

This chapter requires a fundamental knowledge of the relational model Codd [1970] and a preliminary understanding of relational algebra. We briefly introduce the basic definitions and notations, but refer the reader to a relevant textbook [Abiteboul et al., 1995] for an exhaustive introduction to relational databases.

A *relation* is a table identified by a name and a set of *attributes* from a finite universe $\mathcal{U} = \{A_1, ..., A_m\}$ of possible attributes.

A *database schema* is a finite nonempty set of relation names $\{R_1, ..., R_n\}$ and *relation schemas R[U]* identified by the set of attributes. Each attribute A takes values from an infinite set **dom**[1] called the *domain*.

Example 2.2   The Baseball database in Figure 2.1 contains four relations $\{Master, Salary, Team, Batting\}$. Each relation is identified by its name and set of attributes. For instance, the relation Master is represented by *Master[pID, name, country, weight, bat, throw]*. The database schema is depicted in Figure 2.2.

Master

pID	Name	Country	Weight	Bat	Throw
P1	A	U.S.	85	R	L
P2	B	U.S.	72	R	R
P3	C	U.S.	80	R	L
P4	D	Germany	72	L	R
P5	E	Japan	72	R	R

Batting

pID	Year	Stint	Team	HR
P1	2001	2	PIT	40
P1	2003	2	MLI	50
P2	2001	1	PIT	73
P2	2002	1	PIT	40
P3	2004	2	CHA	35
P4	2001	3	PIT	30
P5	2004	3	CHA	60

Salary

pID	Year	Salary
P1	2003	80
P3	2002	35
P5	2004	60

Team

Team	Year	Rank
PIT	2001	7
PIT	2002	4
CHA	2004	3

Figure 2.1: Baseball statistics database.

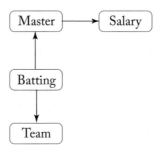

Figure 2.2: Schema graph.

A *relation instance* for a relation R is a set of *tuples* $\{t_1, ..., t_r\}$. A *tuple* in the relation instance of R is a total mapping u from $R[U]$ to **dom**, and is represented as a sequence $\langle A_1 : v_1, ..., A_r : v_r \rangle$. Typically, attribute values are represented as columns in the relation, and tuples as rows. A *database instance* is a set of relation instances. In the example in Figure 2.1, the tuple corresponding to the first row of the relation *Salary* is $\langle pID : P1, year : 2003, salary : 80 \rangle$.

[1]We adopt the model used in Abiteboul et al. [1995], even though attributes may have different domains.

A relational database allows *queries*, which might entail combinations of the projection, selection, join, and grouping *operators*. Such operators allow conditions on the resulting tuples on specific attributes (projection), filtering attribute values (selection), connecting multiple relations (join), and aggregating tuples by values and computing statistics (grouping). The answer of a query Q on the database $\mathcal{D}$ is the set $Q(\mathcal{D})$ of tuples satisfying the conditions in Q.

2.2   REVERSE ENGINEERING QUERIES (REQ)

Reverse engineering queries studies the problem of inferring the SQL query that returns the answers the user provides as an example [Tran et al., 2014]. This approach avoids the daunting task of formulating a query by allowing the user to provide few examples of values that constitute a subset of the intended result. The intended result of a query is a set of tuples T in a relational database $\mathcal{D}$. Reverse engineering queries (REQ) aims at discovering a set of queries $\mathcal{Q}$ (if possible) that produce the results (or a superset of) $Q(\mathcal{D})$ of an unknown query Q, or a set of k queries from $\mathcal{Q}$.

Problem 2.3   Reverse engineering queries   Given a relational database $\mathcal{D}$, a set of tuples T, return a set of k queries $\mathcal{Q} = \{Q_1, ..., Q_k\}$ such that the answers $Q_1(\mathcal{D}), ..., Q_k(\mathcal{D})$ to such queries are *approximately* or *exactly* the tuples in T, i.e., $Q_i(\mathcal{D}) \approx T, i = 1, ..., k$.

During the last few years, we have witnessed a proliferation of REQ methods. The approaches differ on whether the queries return approximately, or precisely the set of example tuples, and on the different query operators considered on the reverse engineering process. For compactness, we represent each query with relational algebra notation; a complete description of relational algebra can be found in Garcia-Molina [2008]. A problem related to that of REQ is the generation of databases for testing using the results of a query as input [Binnig et al., 2007a,b]. However, the generation of test-databases does not provide the ground for exploratory analytics, but rather for algorithm testing. In the following sections, we offer an overview of the main REQ methods. A taxonomy of the different approaches is shown in Figure 2.3.

2.2.1   EXACT REVERSE ENGINEERING

In cases like debugging, query optimization, or database understanding, there is the need to find a set of queries that strictly return those answers with no missing or extra elements in the answer-set. Exact methods can return the queries once in one step [Tran et al., 2009, 2014, Weiss and Cohen, 2017, Zhang et al., 2013], or may engage the user in an interactive refinement approach [Li et al., 2015a]. In the first case, the output is the set of queries that return the examples the user provided, while in the second, the user can refine the set of queries that were returned by providing feedback.

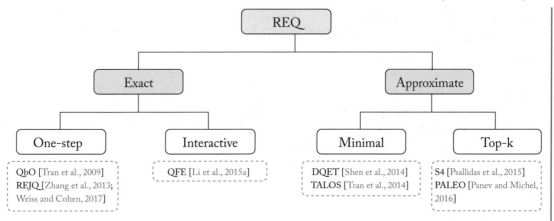

Figure 2.3: Reverse Engineering Queries (REQ).

One-Step Approaches

Query by Output (QbO) [Tran et al., 2009] is the first attempt to solve REQ. Query by Output aims at finding a set of instance-equivalent queries $Q' \equiv_{\mathcal{D}} Q$. Two queries are instance equivalent if they produce the same output on a database $\mathcal{D}$, i.e., $Q'(\mathcal{D}) = Q(\mathcal{D})$. Finding instance-equivalent queries is hard even if restricted to selection and projection predicates [Weiss and Cohen, 2017].

Example 2.4 Figure 2.1 shows a sample database of baseball statistics about players, teams, salaries, team ranks. In particular, the Batting table (b) contains the seasons, the number of home runs (HR), the teams and the year. The user provides the tuples identifying two players (B,PIT) and (E, CHA). Instance equivalent queries are

- $Q_1 = \pi_{country}(\sigma_{bat='R' \wedge throw='R'}(Master))$,

- $Q_2 = \pi_{country}(\sigma_{bat='R' \wedge weight \leq 72}(Master))$, and

- $Q_3 = \pi_{country}(\sigma_{bat='R'}(Master))$.

In its core, Query by Output searches the schema of the database for *core relations* that are necessary to return the results $Q(\mathcal{D})$ of the unknown query Q. The schema of the database can be represented as a *schema graph* of relations connected through foreign-keys. For instance, the schema graph for the database in Figure 2.1 is the one in Figure 2.2. With such intuitive representation, a set of join operations can be defined as a subgraph in the schema graph. Any addition to such subgraphs is a different query to be considered. Algorithm 2.1 illustrates the main steps to return the set of instance-equivalent queries $\mathcal{Q}$. Once the subgraphs are retrieved, the join relations are computed for each subgraph (Line 6).

Algorithm 2.1 Query by Output

Input: Query Q, database $\mathcal{D}$, $Q(\mathcal{D})$
Output: REQ queries $\mathcal{Q}$
  1: $S \leftarrow$ Core relations of Q
  2: $\mathcal{Q} \leftarrow \emptyset$
  3: **for each** schema subgraph G that contains S **do**
  4:    $J \leftarrow$ JoinRelations(G)
  5:    $DT \leftarrow$ EnumerateDecisionTrees(J)
  6:    **for each** $DT \in DT$ **do**
  7:      $Q' \leftarrow$ QueryFromTree(DT)
  8:      $\mathcal{Q} \leftarrow \mathcal{Q} \cup \{Q'\}$
  9:    **end for**
10: **end for**

After having determined the join relations, the algorithm needs to find the selection conditions (e.g., *weight*$\leq$72). Enumerating all possible selection conditions is infeasible because of a large number of combinations. However, the problem can be cast as learning a decision boundary. More specifically, after joining the tables, all the user's tuples T are marked as positives and the remaining as negatives. In this way, the problem translates to finding a decision tree DT that correctly retains the positive tuples and none of the negative ones (Line 5). If such a tree exists, the valid queries Q' are obtained by traversing the tree from the root to the leaves (Line 7–8). Figure 2.4a shows a (simplified) example for a join table $J = Master\bowtie Batting\bowtie Team$ for the user tuples $T=\{(B,PIT), (E,CHA)\}$. Tuples t_5 and t_6 match (B,PIT), while tuple t_7 matches (E, CHA), the remaining are marked as negative (✗). Figure 2.4b shows one tree corresponding the join table J: the decision tree represents potential queries such as $Q' = \pi_{name}\sigma_{stint>1 \wedge HR>50)}(J)$, which returns the tuple $Q'(\mathcal{D}) = \{t_7\}$.

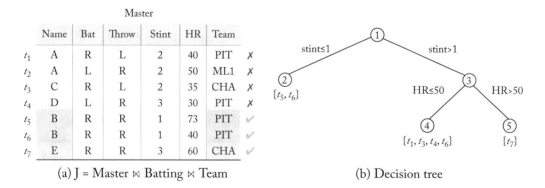

	Name	Bat	Throw	Stint	HR	Team	
t_1	A	R	L	2	40	PIT	✗
t_2	A	L	R	2	50	ML1	✗
t_3	C	R	L	2	35	CHA	✗
t_4	D	L	R	3	30	PIT	✗
t_5	B	R	R	1	73	PIT	✔
t_6	B	R	R	1	40	PIT	✔
t_7	E	R	R	3	60	CHA	✔

(a) J = Master ⋈ Batting ⋈ Team   (b) Decision tree

Figure 2.4: A simplified join table and decision tree for $T=\{(B,PIT), (E,CHA)\}$.

Reverse Engineering Complex Join Queries (REJQ) [Zhang et al., 2013] extends QbO semantics to return all the possible join relations given the user tuples T. The method builds on the idea of the schema graph, and instead of constraining the joins to a path in the graph, the method returns complex join relations (walks).

Example 2.5   Consider for instance the query on the database in Figure 2.1 asking for pairs of player names that belong to the same team. Such a query requires to join twice on the tables *Master* and *Batting* and, as such, cannot be represented as a path on the schema graph in Figure 2.2, but rather with a walk Master1—Batting—Master2, where *Master1* and *Master2* are copies of the *Master* relation.

As the example above shows, enumerating all the possible walks to find complex join queries is unfeasible: there is no way to know when to stop traversing the same tables multiple times, i.e., the algorithm would walk in a loop. REJQ remedies to this problem with a natural observation: complex joins can be seen as an aggregation of multiple join paths with a common central table, called a *star*. In the previous example, two Master—Batting paths are aggregated into one.

Once all the stars are returned, simpler queries are obtained by merging nodes that correspond to duplicate tables. For instance, the join query Q' : $\boxed{\text{Master1}} \bowtie Batting \bowtie \boxed{\text{Master2}}$, can be merged into the query Q'' : $\boxed{\text{Master}} \bowtie Batting$. Queries are generated by merge operations within a *lattice of queries* with the star query on top and the queries obtained by one merge operation in each level. As such, the number of queries in the lattice is exponential in the number of copies of the tables in the star graph. Queries generated by merging return progressively fewer tuples due to the more restrictive conditions. In particular, if Q'' is a merge of Q' $Q''(\mathcal{D}) \subseteq Q'(\mathcal{D})$. This observation yields to the early pruning of redundant and uninformative queries.

In the last step, REJQ verifies whether a generated query Q' returns exactly the example tuples, i.e., it checks whether $T \stackrel{?}{=} Q'(\mathcal{D})$. If the verification check succeeds, Q' is added into the set of the returned queries $\mathcal{Q}$. The overview of the REJQ procedure is presented in Algorithm 2.2.

Iterative Approaches

An iterative approach drives the user toward the definition of a query through simple steps. Query From Examples (QFE) [Li et al., 2015a] considers this as a key aspect and proposes a method that restricts the (potentially large) set of queries returned by traditional methods. Consider as input examples the players A and C from Figure 2.1, hence the example tuples are $T=\{A, C\}$. For simplicity, we consider a database containing only the table Master. Possible queries returning T are

- $Q_1 = \sigma_{throw='L'}(Master)$,

Algorithm 2.2 Reverse Engineering Complex Join Queries

Input: Query Q, database $\mathcal{D}$, $Q(\mathcal{D})$, max distance d_{max}
Output: REQ queries $\mathcal{Q}$
 1: **while** $d < d_{max}$ **do**
 2:    Compute schema walks of some length d
 3:    Create stars from valid walks that return the tuples T
 4:    Create the lattice merging nodes in each star
 5:    Test each query Q' whether $T = Q'(\mathcal{D})$
 6: **end while**

- $Q_2 = \sigma_{weight \geq 80}(Master)$,

- and $Q_3 = \sigma_{country='USA' \wedge weight > 72}(Master)$.

What is the best way to select the query for the user?

QFE offers a simple but effective interaction with the user, based on a *modified database* $\mathcal{D}'$, and the results obtained by the queries $\mathcal{Q}$ updated according to $\mathcal{D}'$. A modified database is a database in which values of some tuples are altered to exclude some of the proposed queries $\mathcal{Q}$. Consider the new database $\mathcal{D}'$ in Figure 2.5a, the weight of player P3 has been changed from 80 to 79. In this way, query Q_2 (Figure 2.5b) returns only tuple A. The modified database and the updated resultsets are then presented to the user. The user is then invited to select the desired resultset among those of each query in the new database $\mathcal{D}'$. If the user selects $Q_2(\mathcal{D}')$ then the system can infer that the only correct query is Q_2. Otherwise, the database is modified again until only one query is selected. The entire process clearly terminates, since the set of queries is reduced at each iteration.

pID	Name	Country	Weight	Bat	Throw
P1	A	U.S.	85	R	L
P2	B	U.S.	72	R	R
P3	C	U.S.	79	R	L
P4	D	Germany	72	L	R
P5	E	Japan	72	R	R

$Q_1 = \sigma_{throw='L'}(\mathcal{D}')$ $Q_1(\mathcal{D}')=\{A, C\}$
$Q_2 = \sigma_{weight \geq 80}(\mathcal{D}')$ $Q_2(\mathcal{D}')=\{A\}$
$Q_3 = \sigma_{country='U.S.' \atop \wedge weight > 72}(\mathcal{D}')$ $Q_3(\mathcal{D}')=\{A, C\}$

(a) Modified database $\mathcal{D}'$ (b) Queries and results on $\mathcal{D}$

Figure 2.5: A modified db (a); the queries and their validity on tuples $T = A, C$ (b).

In short, the QFE approach entails two steps that are interleaved with the user feedback: (1) query generation and (2) database generation.

(1) *Query generation* initially takes the database $\mathcal{D}$, and the examples T and returns reverse engineered queries. Any one-step approach for reverse engineering serves the purpose; QFE uses Query by Output [Tran et al., 2009] to compute the query.

(2) *Database generation* generates a new database from the queries $\mathcal{Q}$ computed in the previous step. The purpose of query generation is to find a database which partitions the queries $\mathcal{Q}$ into k subsets $\mathcal{Q}_1, ..., \mathcal{Q}_k$, for which the modified database is similar to the original database $\mathcal{D}$. There is an exponential number of databases that can be generated from the initial one. As such, Li et al. [2015a] propose a cost function based on the overhead of editing the existing database and the future overhead. The cost is computed as

$$C(\mathcal{D}') = \underbrace{\delta(\mathcal{D}, \mathcal{D}') + \beta \cdot n}_{\text{Database cost}} + \underbrace{\sum_{i=1}^{k} \delta(T, Q_i(\mathcal{D}'))}_{\text{Results cost}} + \underbrace{N \frac{\delta(\mathcal{D}, \mathcal{D}')}{\mu} + \beta}_{\text{Checkup } \mathcal{D}'} + \underbrace{\frac{2}{k} \sum_{i=1}^{k} \delta(T, Q_i(\mathcal{D}'))}_{\text{Checkup results}},$$

where δ is an edit distance computed on the tuples, n is the number of modified tuples, $N = \log_2 \max\{|\mathcal{Q}_1|, ..., |\mathcal{Q}_k|\}$ is an upper bound of the number of iterations to find the correct query, μ is the number of modified tuples, and β is a normalization parameter. Since finding a database $\mathcal{D}'$ that minimizes the cost is hard, QFE adopts a multi-objective (skyline) approach that maximizes each of the individual costs independently and generates databases that have minimum individual costs among those four.

Exact Reverse Engineering Complexity

Finding queries that return exactly the set of results the user wants is intuitively a hard task. Recently, work by Weiss and Cohen [2017] addressed the question on how hard that is and found that REQ's time complexity depends on the relational operators to infer and on the limits on the size of the query, the number of joins (or tables), and the number of examples provided. Intuitively, constraints might pose additional challenges or restrict the search and simplify the solution. Furthermore, the complexity changes whenever the constraint is a constant or part of the input since the complexity grows with input size. Figure 2.6 shows the complexity of each operator when the size of the query is not bounded.

Similarly, Weiss and Cohen [2017] reports complexity analysis for bounded queries, where the size of the query is a number k. In the case of bounded queries, the complexity typically increases as the problem reduces to Cover problems (Set-Cover, Vertex-Cover). For instance, returning a query of bounded size allowing only the select (σ) operator reduces to find a subset of attributes that covers the entire set of examples (Set-Cover) which is **NP**-complete. However, if the query is constant, the problem becomes polynomial as the exponent in the complexity is fixed.

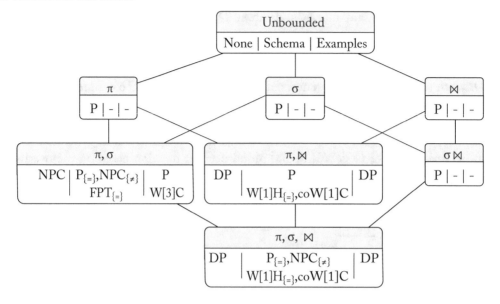

Figure 2.6: Complexity classes for unbounded queries and different query operators ($\pi, \sigma, \bowtie$). For each node in the lattice, we report the complexity when we constrain none of the input (first column), only the number of joins (second colmun), or only the number of examples (third column). The last row of each node shows the complexity when the constraints are treated as input as opposed to constants (second row). The complexity for $=, \neq$ conditions in joins or selections are reported separately.

2.2.2   APPROXIMATE REVERSE ENGINEERING

As analyzed previously, finding a query that exactly returns the examples the user provides is often impractical or even impossible. Approximate reverse engineering has been proposed to address the rigidity of the exact approaches in the previous section, yet deviating minimally from the user input. Approximate methods either return the closest query to the user examples (minimal queries) [Shen et al., 2014] or k queries which can approximately return the user examples (top-k) queries [Panev and Michel, 2016, Psallidas et al., 2015].

Minimal Queries
Shen et al. [2014] proposed the first solution for approximate reverse engineering of queries. To allow more flexible combinations of queries, instead of a set of tuples, the user provides an example table. An *example table* is a table where each cell might be filled with a value or left empty. Given an example table T, a *valid* Project-Join Query is a query Q such that there exists

a mapping from the attributes in T to the columns in the database $\mathcal{D}$ for each row in T and each column, the corresponding mapped attribute contains the value of the said column.

Example 2.6   Consider the example in Figure 2.7, where is represented the database for a computer retailer which also provides repair services for employees. A user possesses partial information about customer names, devices, and the application used, but does not know how to find the rest with a query. Shen et al. [2014] respond to this need by using the partial information of the table in Figure 2.7b to derive a set of queries. Such set of queries is depicted at the bottom of Figure 2.7b.

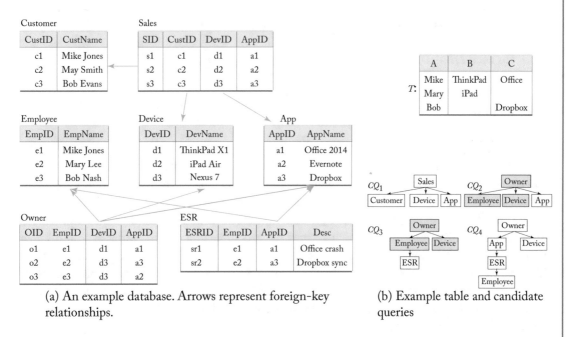

(a) An example database. Arrows represent foreign-key relationships.

(b) Example table and candidate queries

Figure 2.7: (a) A database of a computer retailer, (b) an example table and the candidate reverese queries.

There is a considerable number of queries that can be generated, but a closer look reveals substantial redundancies. In particular, column A in Figure 2.7b can refer to both attributes CustName and EmpName; however, one of the attributes is redundant. Therefore, it is important to focus on minimal queries: a **valid** query Q is *minimal* if every column is mapped in the database exactly once. Shen et al. [2014] provide a solution to the problem of efficiently discovering minimal project join queries (MPJQ) given an example table T.

The solution for MPJQ entails two steps (described in Algorithm 2.3). First, a set of minimal candidate queries are generated; second, a verification removes queries that are not valid. While generation and verification can be done separately, such an approach can potentially discover a large set of invalid queries which could be removed with a smart pruning. In the example above, out of the four candidate queries $CQ_1, ..., CQ_4$ only CQ_1 is valid, the others, by joining the table Owner, invalidate the second row of example table T.

Algorithm 2.3 Minimal Project Joing Queries

Input: Query Q, database $\mathcal{D}$, $Q(\mathcal{D})$
Output: REQ queries $\mathcal{Q}$
1: $S \leftarrow$ Core relations of Q
2: $\mathcal{Q} \leftarrow \emptyset$
3: **for each** schema subgraph G that contains S **do**
4:    $J \leftarrow$ JoinRelations(G)
5:    $DT \leftarrow$ EnumerateDecisionTrees(J)
6:    **for each** $DT \in DT$ **do**
7:       $Q' \leftarrow$ QueryFromTree(DT)
8:       $\mathcal{Q} \leftarrow \mathcal{Q} \cup \{Q'\}$
9:    **end for**
10: **end for**

A better approach for MPJQ considers redundancies of the overlapping structures in the query trees. For instance, the subtree Owner-Employee-Device is common in query CQ_2 and CQ_3 in Figure 2.7b. By observing common structures, one can prune queries faster: if the validation in the subtree fails, then both CQ_2 and CQ_3 are invalid. As a further speedup, MPJQ proposes an adaptive verification which verifies substructures in a specific order as to minimize the number of validations. Finding a sequence that minimizes the number of validation is hard since even if the valid/invalid substructures are known finding the minimum number of selection corresponds to solving the SET-COVER problem [Karp, 1972]. The adopted solution is greedy, in that it selects at each iteration the substructure which is contained in the maximum number of candidate queries.

Top-k Queries

MPJQ returns queries whose answer contains the entire example table T and potentially additional other tuples. MPJQ presumes that the user is aware on some tuples of the database and is interested in completing the results with an unknown query. On the other hand, exploratory analytics often enjoy more substantial freedom in the specifications, in a way that the results are only partially returned, but the user has a better understanding of the data. S4 [Psallidas et al., 2015] targets the exploratory intent and proposes a top-k approach for example-based query reverse engineering.

The main idea driving S4 is that a candidate query can return some columns or some rows of the example table T without returning complete tuples. In this regard, S4 builds upon MPJQ assigning a score $score(T|Q)$ to each query Q. Such score is a linear combination of a row similarity $score_{row}(T|Q)$ and a column similarity $score_{col}(T|Q)$ between the results of the query $Q(\mathcal{D})$ and the example table T

$$score(T|Q) = \frac{\alpha \cdot score_{row}(T|Q) + (1-\alpha) \cdot score_{col}(T|Q)}{1 + \ln(1 + \ln|Q|)}, \qquad (2.1)$$

where the size of the query $|Q|$ is the number of joined tables and $\alpha \in [0, 1]$ regulates the importance of the row and the column similarity. A value of α close to 1 penalizes missing rows, while as α approaches 0 missing columns are penalized. In this way, the relative importance of the reverse queries can fit different purposes and datasets.

The row similarity expresses how many rows of the example table T are correctly returned by the query Q and is expressed as

$$score_{row}(T|Q) = \sum_{t \in T} \max_{r \in Q(\mathcal{D})} score(t|r), \qquad (2.2)$$

where $score(t|r)$ sums the similarity of the individual cells of the tuples with the corresponding (mapped) cells in the row r in the results $Q(\mathcal{D})$. The cell similarity can be then computed exactly, i.e., by comparing the strings, or with approximate similarities among strings and values [Gomaa and Fahmy, 2013]. The motivation to compute the maximum score lays in the possibility to return more tuples than those in the example table. Similarly, the column similarity is computed on each column and cell in the columns of T. The computation of the score for query CQ_1 is shown in Figure 2.8. Finally, S4 returns a set of k minimal project-join queries that have the smallest overall score.

Since the enumeration of all the project-join queries is impractical, S4 computes an upper bound on the row-score, based on the column store. In fact, the row-score cannot be larger than the column score which does not take into account the sequence of values in the example tuples. Moreover, the search for the minimal project-join queries can be reduced further by reasoning on trees and subtrees as in MPJQ and fast caching of subtrees. Such a strategy allows in the experiments by Psallidas et al. [2015] the computation of results in less than 1 s.

Top-k Aggregation Queries
Until now, we have discussed algorithms in which the query operators are restricted to project (π), select (σ), and join ($\bowtie$). A natural extension is to consider also aggregation such as average, maximum, minimum, and sum. This scenario arises when a user has proposed the top-k items with respect to some criteria. For instance, in the database in Figure 2.1, we can consider a list of players and their maximum HR (home-run rate) is returned. Such queries require an aggregation over the Batting table.

PALEO [Panev and Michel, 2016] proposes a solution to the problem of reverse engineering database queries when the input is a set of k items with a ranking value.

PALEO takes as input a table L with two columns, a list of items and a value for each item, and computes a query Q which returns the items in the same order and aggregated using the

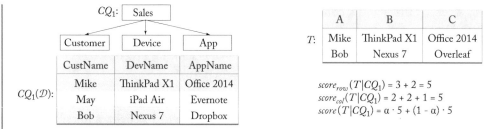

$score_{row}(T|CQ_1) = 3 + 2 = 5$
$score_{col}(T|CQ_1) = 2 + 2 + 1 = 5$
$score(T|CQ_1) = \alpha \cdot 5 + (1 - \alpha) \cdot 5$

(a) A query and its results   (b) Example table and scores for query CQ_1

Figure 2.8: Scores computed in S4 for an example table.

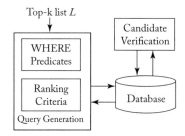

Figure 2.9: The PALEO system.

value. PALEO selects the tuples in the database matching the items in L and generates *candidate queries* selecting first the right predicates in the WHERE clause and then in the ranking criteria. Finally, PALEO validates the candidate queries on the database. Figure 2.9 shows the steps and components of the PALEO system.

Challenges and Future Directions: Although the advancements in query reverse engineering have paved a path toward systems requiring little or no user expertise in query languages by allowing example-based approaches, no commercial system supports such semantics. On the research side, while REQ shows maturity in the solutions, it still lacks proper benchmarks for testing the results on different hardness. In particular, no solution considers the hardness of examples provided as input. Moreover, indexes and other structures are hardly taken into account. A missing tile in current solutions is a user model which explicitly embraces the differences and the preferences of users. If such a model is integrated, better results could be achieved with techniques similar to query refinement and interactive query formulation [Dimitriadou et al., 2016, Mishra and Koudas, 2009, Mottin et al., 2013].

2.3   SCHEMA MAPPING

Interactive example-based methods found application besides query reverse engineering. In particular, they have been employed in complex tasks, such as schema mapping, where the human intervention is beneficial or even unavoidable. The natural specification through examples applies to other tasks as well, such as explaining and mapping tuples in databases with different schemas [Popa et al., 2002, Yan et al., 2001].

Definition 2.7   A *schema mapping* is a correspondence $\mathcal{M} = (\mathbf{S}, \mathbf{T}, \Sigma)$ between the attributes in the schema $\mathbf{S}$ of a *source* database and the schema $\mathbf{T}$ of a target database. In a mapping $\mathcal{M}$, Σ is a set of specifications denoted with $\phi_1 \rightarrow \phi_2$, where ϕ_1, ϕ_2 are first-order logic formulas on the attributes of $\mathbf{S}$ and $\mathbf{T}$, respectively.

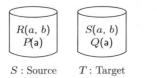

$$\mathcal{M}_1 : \forall xy(R(x,y) \rightarrow S(x,y)), \forall x(P(x) \rightarrow Q(x))$$
$$\mathcal{M}_2 : \forall xy(R(x,y) \wedge P(x) \rightarrow S(x,y)),$$
$$\forall xy(R(x,y) \wedge P(x) \rightarrow Q(x))$$
$$\mathcal{M}_3 : \forall xy(R(x,y) \rightarrow S(x,y) \wedge Q(x))$$

S : Source T : Target

Figure 2.10: **A** source and target database schema and candidate schema mapping from source to target.

Example 2.8   Consider the two sample databases in Figure 2.10. The source database contains two tables, R and P; the target database other two tables S and Q. Multiple mappings are possible among these two databases. Mapping $\mathcal{M}_1$ for instance maps every tuple in R with a tuple in S, and every tuple in P with a tuple in Q. This mapping does not preserve the foreign key in S and Q, which is maintained by $\mathcal{M}_2$ and $\mathcal{M}_3$. Mapping $\mathcal{M}_3$, on the other hand, is the smallest mapping which preserves the global and local views on the source database.

This section presents a compendium of *example-driven schema mapping* techniques which are not intended to be exhaustive but to give an idea of the flexibility of examples for solving more complex tasks in the relational domain. These techniques are beneficial in an exploration setting because it helps in exploring an unfamiliar database T by identifying correspondences in the contents of a more familiar database S. Ten Cate et al. [2013] presented an exhaustive tutorial on example-driven schema mapping solutions. We analyze two different strategies: the generation of examples from schema mapping for explanation, and the example-driven schema mapping.

2.3.1   FROM SCHEMA MAPPING TO EXAMPLES

A first family of methods generates data examples to explain complex mappings. A *Data example* is a pair (I, J) of databases I from the source schema $\mathbf{S}$ and J from the target schema $\mathbf{T}$. A *uniquely characterizing set of data examples* is a set of data example in which there is only one schema mapping that "fits" the set of data examples. Such works, more notably the one by Alexe et al. [2011a], assume the schema mapping is already provided, which is a prerogative of expert users. Alexe et al. [2011a] provides the foundation and the characterization of the examples required to explain a mapping between two datasets, but do not develop the idea how to return possible mappings for a set of examples. As such, we do not expand on such techniques further.

Remark 2.9   The name data example might be confusing. In this case, it is defined as a pair of data instances or a dataset and not a pair of tuples as previously used.

2.3.2   EXAMPLE-DRIVEN SCHEMA MAPPING

Instead of providing a data example for an already existing schema mapping, example-driven schema mapping discovers the relationships among the datasets via the input user examples. Approaches for example-driven schema mapping can require the user to provide one or more data examples [Alexe et al., 2011b, Cate et al., 2013, Gottlob and Senellart, 2010] or ask questions on the validity of the generated mapping based on few exemplar tuples [Bonifati et al., 2016]. The latter approach tends to advantage user interactions, while the first requires a fully specified pair of datasets to map the source to the target scheme.

Schema Mapping Based on Data Examples

Schema mapping based on data examples requires the user to provide datasets from the source and the target schema as examples. EIRENE [Alexe et al., 2011b] takes a fitting approach on the data examples and return the most general fitting schema to such examples. Gottlob and Senellart [2010] finds a schema mapping with a minimal cost, where the cost is defined on the size of the schema mapping and how well it fits the data example. Cate et al. [2013] applies statistical learning theories to determine the power and the limitations of the algorithmic methods for obtaining schema mapping from data examples.

EIRENE [Alexe et al., 2011b] finds the smallest schema mapping given a certain *universal* data example (I, J). A universal data example J is the "most general" solution for I given a global and local (GLAV) schema mapping $\mathcal{M} = (\mathbf{S}, \mathbf{T}, \Sigma)$. Testing whether a fitting GLAV exists is Π_2^P-complete. If such schema mapping exists its construction requires polynomial time by taking the conjunction of the facts in I on the left-hand side of the mapping specification and the conjunction of the facts in J on the right-hand side of the specification. Conversely, if no mapping exists, the user can correct the data examples.

Gottlob–Senellart (GS) [Gottlob and Senellart, 2010] takes an optimization approach which returns a mapping with a minimal cost with respect to a data example (I, J). Assuming a mapping $\mathcal{M}$ which does not fit a data example, GS defines a "repair" language which refines such mapping until the repaired mapping fits the data example. However, the space of the possible repairs is exponential. Therefore, GS defines a *cost* as the size of the smallest repair that fits the data example. GS than returns the mapping with the minimum repairing cost. GS, as opposed to EIRENE, is always guaranteed to find a valid mapping.

Example 2.10   Consider the data example ($I = \{R(a_1, b_1), R(a_2, b_2), R(a_3, b_3), R(a_4, b_4)\}$, $J = \{S(a_1, c_1), S(a_2, c_2), S(a_3, c_3), S(d, e)\}$) and the mapping $R(x, y) \to \exists z S(x, z)$. Such mapping excludes $S(d, e)$ which is instead part of the data example. A possible repaired schema mapping which fits the data example is $R(x, y) \land x \neq a_4 \to \exists z S(x, z) \bigwedge_i (x = a_i \to z = c_i), S(d, e)$.

The repair procedure takes a GLAV schema mapping $\mathcal{M}$ and (1) extends its left-hand side with additional conditions of the form $x = c$ and $x \neq c$, (2) extends its right-hand side with conditions of the form $(x_a = c_1 \land ... \land x_n = c_n) \to y = d$, (3) adds the ground facts to the schema mapping (i.e., facts on the relations).

The *size* of the repaired schema mapping is the number of occurrences of variables and constant symbols, where ground facts $R(a_1, ..., a_n)$ have size $3n$ since the formula can be thought as $\exists x_1...\exists x_n R(x_1...x_n) \land x_1 = c_1 \land ... \land x_n = c_n$.

Example 2.11   Consider the repair $\Sigma_1 = R(x, y) \land x \neq a_4 \to \exists z S(x, z) \bigwedge_i (x = a_i \to z = c_i), S(d, e)$ in Example 2.10; its size is $|\Sigma_1| = \underbrace{3 \cdot 2 + 2}_{R(x,y) \land x \neq a_4} + \underbrace{3 \cdot 2 + 4}_{\exists z S(x,z)...} + \underbrace{3 \cdot 2}_{S(d,e)} = 24$.

The *cost* $cost_{(I,J)}(\mathcal{M})$ of a schema mapping $\mathcal{M}$ with data example (I, J) is the size of the smallest repair of $\mathcal{M}$ fitting (I, J). Finally, the problem of GS is the following. Given a data example (I, J) find a schema mapping $\mathcal{M}*$ such that the $cost_{(I,J)}(\mathcal{M}*)$ is minimum

$$\mathcal{M}* = \underset{\mathcal{M}}{\operatorname{argmin}} \, cost_{(I,J)}(\mathcal{M}).$$

Gottlob and Senellart [2010] proves that such problem is hard under different conditions, like finding a mapping with $cost_{(I,J)}(\mathcal{M}) < k$ (Π_2^p-hard), or finding schema mapping without existential ($\exists$) quantifiers (Π_2^p-hard and *DP*-hard), while corresponding decision problems are **NP**-hard.

Schema Mapping Based on Exemplar Tuples

Among the different methods for schema mapping, the one proposed by Bonifati et al. [2017] is the only one that engages the user in an interactive process to return schema mappings for any database. This approach explicitly targets novice users allowing them to specify tuples E_S from the source databases and E_T from the target database. The tuples are employed in the generation of an initial rigid mapping, which is subsequently refined and relaxed by asking simple Boolean questions to the user. The overall process is always guaranteed to produce a mapping $\mathcal{M}'$ which generalizes an undisclosed mapping $\mathcal{M}$ in the user's mind. The flow of Bonifati et al. [2017] approach is depicted in Figure 2.11.

The refinement procedure in Figure 2.11 involves two separate steps: atom refinement and join refinement. Atom refinement simplifies the left-hand side of the initially generated rule by exploring the lattice of all possible atoms and pruning those that are invalidated by the user. Join refinement takes each rule generated by atom refinement, identifies redundant joins entailed by multiple occurrences of a given variable, and asks the user about the validity of small sets of tuples.

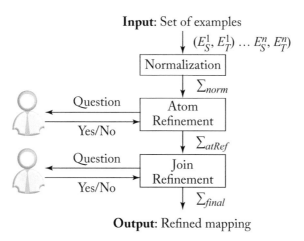

Input: Set of examples
$(E_S^1, E_T^1) \dots E_S^n, E_T^n)$

Normalization

Σ_{norm}

Question
Yes/No
Atom Refinement

Σ_{atRef}

Question
Yes/No
Join Refinement

Σ_{final}

Output: Refined mapping

Figure 2.11: Interactive schema mapping (based on Bonifati et al. [2017]).

Challenges and Future Directions: Schema mapping using examples shows that example-based approaches can substantially help the definition and the solution of complex tasks with intuitive inputs. The need for more specialized solutions should go beyond a few data tasks. Among all the methods, the Bonifati et al. [2017] is the only one that engages the user in the mapping process, while the others assume that at least a source and a target database is available. However, such mapping specification seeks for global mappings instead of localized approaches in some parts of the database.

Moreover, mapping algorithms allow no error or approximations. An interesting question is whether more approximate mappings could be returned, even if the database is incomplete or noisy.

2.4   DATA CLEANING

Data cleaning [Ganti and Sarma, 2013] refers to practices and techniques that, once applied to a given dataset, enforce the consistency of the values, the attributes, and the schema. Data cleaning practices assess the validity, the accuracy, the completeness, the consistency, and the uniformity of the data. Preserving such properties requires an extensive knowledge of the data and the schema. While example-based methods facilitate daunting data cleaning tasks, there has been little development in said area. We describe two works in the area which perform entity matching (Section 2.4.1) and data repairing (Section 2.4.2) involving the user in the process.

2.4.1 ENTITY MATCHING

Entity matching (EM) is one of the steps of Entity Resolution [Christophides et al., 2015, Papadakis and Palpanas, 2018, Papadakis et al., 2015, 2016, 2018], which refers to methods designed to find mentions of the same entities across different databases (a.k.a. record linkage), or duplicates in the same database (a.k.a. deduplication). EM is the step of the process that estimates the similarity of candidate matches, and several of the proposed methods rely on example matching/non-matching tuples, or handcrafted rules that define how to match values among different tuples.

Example 2.12   Consider the database in Figure 2.12 with two relations $R(\textbf{name}, \textbf{adress}, \textbf{email}, \textbf{nation}, \textbf{gender})$ and $S(\textbf{name}, \textbf{apt}, \textbf{email}, \textbf{country}, \textbf{sex})$. A possible EM rule can be:

$$\varphi_1 : r[\textbf{name}] \approx_1 s[\textbf{name}] \wedge r[\textbf{address}] \approx_2 s[\textbf{apt}] \wedge r[\textbf{email}] = s[\textbf{email}]$$
$$\wedge\, r[\textbf{nation}] \approx s[\textbf{country}] \wedge r[\textbf{gender}] \approx s[\textbf{sex}],$$

where $\approx_1$ and $\approx_2$ are potentially two different similarity functions among the values in the tuples (e.g., edit distance). The rule φ_1 returns true if the values in all the mentioned attributes are equal or similar.

Instance of Schema R

	Name	Address	Email	Nation	Gender
r_1	Catherine Z.-Jones	9601 Wilshire, Beverly Hills, CA, 90210	c.jones@a.com	Wales	F
r_2	C. Zeta-Jones	3rd Floor, Beverly Hills, CA, 90210	c.jones@a.com	U.S.	F
r_3	Michael Jordan	Michigan Avenue, Suite 2913, Chicago		U.S.	M
r_4	Bob Dylan	Avenue of the Americas, NY, 10020		U.S.	M

Instance of Schema S

	Name	Apt	Email	Nation	Sex
s_1	Catherine Z.-Jones	3rd Floor, Beverly Hills, CA, 90210	c.jones@a.com	Wales	F
s_2	B. Dylan	Avenue of the Americas, NY, 10020	bob.dylan@a.com	U.S.	M
s_3	Michael Jordan	Evans Hall, Berkley, CA 94720	j@cs.berkley.edu	U.S.	M

Figure 2.12: A sample database with two relations R and S.

Rule discovery algorithms compute rules directly from the data as opposed to rules provided by domain experts. Among other characteristics, RuleSynth utilizes *General Boolean Formulas* (GBF), a richer logic for rules which express conjunction, disjunctions, and negations. RuleSynth [Singh et al., 2017] is the first example-based approach to rule discovery.

RuleSynth aims at generating an optimal GBF by a set of examples $E = E^+ \cup E^-$, where E^+ is a set of pairs of matching tuples and E^- are negative examples representing different entities.

Problem 2.13 Rule discovery by example Given two relations R and S, a set of positive E^+ and negative E^- examples, similarity functions $\mathcal{F}$ among attributes in the relations, find a GBF Φ that maximizes some metric $q(\Phi, E^+, E^-) \rightarrow [0, 1]$ as a function of Φ and the examples.

RuleSynth first formulates the problem as a Program Synthesis problem. In Program Synthesis [Solar-Lezama, 2009], the aim is to find a program, defined by a particular grammar, which satisfies a set of input-output example (behavioral constraints). Hence, RuleSynth solves the problem using a solver, SKETCH [Solar-Lezama, 2009]. However, SKETCH solves the exact problem in which the examples represent hard constraints that need to be always true. Therefore, SKETCH as-is, cannot solve Problem 2.13. The proposed solution is based on sampling the set of examples E and returns the best formula Φ found with the SKETCH solver. The random samples generate also counter-examples to improve the subset of E and avoiding local optima.

2.4.2 INTERACTIVE DATA REPAIRING

Data repairing aims at detecting and correcting inconsistencies in data. Inconsistencies arise when data is not adequately maintained (updated), or inaccuracies are injected by human intervention or faulty code.

Example 2.14 Consider the dataset in Figure 2.13a representing data from a chemistry laboratory. The marked values have been incorrectly filled in and never updated. Inconsistent datasets are detrimental to the quality of the experiments of that lab. On the other hand, a manual intervention to fix the problem on potentially large datasets is expensive and cumbersome.

FALCON [He et al., 2016] is a data cleaning system that interactively updates inconsistent values in a dirty database. The method relies on rules similar to those used in RuleSynth and human feedback to fix the inconsistencies to the largest extent.

Consider again the inconsistent dataset in Figure 2.13a. A user would like to update the incorrect cells with the values in Figure 2.13b. For instance, to correct the entry t_3, the user should substitute "N. Y." with "New York." Such entry-fix can be represented as $t_3[\text{Laboratory}] \leftarrow$ "New York". However, multiple entries might present the same error, and fixing all of them manually is slow and ineffective.

FALCON proposes an automatic generation of rules that fix inconsistencies in the data, by asking the user to validate only a few of them. FALCON update rules are SQL queries that take an attribute A in a relation T and change its value to a if all the Boolean conditions $X = t[X]$ on a set of attributes X hold on the entries. Such rules are translated into SQL queries in the form

$$\text{UPDATE } T \text{ SET } A = a \text{ WHERE } X = t[X].$$

For instance, a rule for t_2 and t_5 in Figure 2.13a that fixes the molecule name is UPDATE T SET Molecule='$C_{22}H_{28}F$' WHERE Molecule='statin' AND Laboratory='Austin'.

tid	Date	Molecule	Laboratory	Quantity
t_1	11 Nov	$C_{16}H_{16}Cl$	Austin	200
t_2	12 Nov	statin	Austin	100
t_3	12 Nov	$C_{24}H_{75}S_6$	N.Y.	100
t_4	12 Nov	statin	Boston	200
t_5	13 Nov	$C_{22}H_{28}F$	Austin	200
t_6	15 Nov	$C_{17}H_{20}N$	Dubai	1,000

tid	Date	Molecule	Laboratory	Quantity
t_1	11 Nov	$C_{16}H_{16}Cl$	Austin	200
t_2	12 Nov	$C_{22}H_{28}F$	Austin	100
t_3	12 Nov	$C_{24}H_{75}S_6$	New York	100
t_4	12 Nov	$C_{22}H_{28}F$	Boston	200
t_5	13 Nov	$C_{22}H_{28}F$	Austin	200
t_6	15 Nov	$C_{17}H_{20}N$	Dubai	100

(a) Inconsistent table   (b) Corrected table

Figure 2.13: A database of a chemistry lab.

Finding update rules is a hard problem since the number of combinations of attributes and values is exponential even in the case of the *closed-world semantics* that FALCON adopts. Recall that the closed-world semantics assumes that the only valid values for an attribute are those present in the database. As such, the number of interactions with the user should be limited to a budget B, and the benefit of these interactions to repair the dataset is maximized.

Problem 2.15 Budget Repair Problem   Given a set Q of rules, a table T and a budget B, find B rules from Q to maximize the number of repairs over T.

The Budget Repair Problem is **NP**-hard even in the static version, where the rules are provided upfront by reduction from the *Maximum-Coverage* problem [Papadimitriou, 2003]. The proposed solution explores the lattice of the rules obtained from the relation $\preceq$ on the rules. In particular, two rules Q and Q' in the table T are in relation $Q \preceq Q'$ if the tuples entailed by Q are a subset of the tuples entailed by Q', $Q(T) \subseteq Q'(T)$. The $\preceq$ relation determines an effective method to check the validity of the set of rules.

[P1] If Q is valid, all Q' such that $Q' \preceq Q$ are valid.

[P2] If Q is invalid, all Q'' such that $Q \preceq Q''$ are invalid.

A *rule lattice* $(\mathcal{Q}, \preceq)$ is materialized from the $\preceq$ relation by drawing an arrow from Q to Q' if $Q \preceq Q'$. While materializing the entire lattice is impractical even for few attributes and values, the $\preceq$ relation offers a convenient pruning property. FALCON exploits this property by implementing a binary search technique on rules appropriately sampled from the lattice.

The FALCON dive search algorithm (Algorithm 2.4) works iteratively, by asking at most B questions to the user, and drilling down the lattice in a divide-and-conquer fashion.

Algorithm 2.4 FALCON - Dive Search

Input: Budget B, Table T

1: **[Initialization]** Materialize the top Q^+ (more specific) and bottom node Q^- (more generic, no conditions in the WHERE clause) of the lattice, the set $Q^? = \mathcal{Q} \setminus (Q^- \cup Q^+)$ of candidate rules to ask and the set Q_v of rules verified by the user.
2: **while** $B > 0$ **do**
3:    **[Sort]** Sort candidate rules based on the number of affected tuples.
4:    **[Binary jump]** Select the next node Q to ask the user by traversing the lattice on a path from Q.
5:    **if** Q is valid **then**
6:       Update table T with Q and include all $Q' \preceq Q$ into Q^+
7:       Update $Q^??$ with the rules Q'' such that $Q \preceq Q''$
8:    **else**
9:       Update Q^- with the rules Q'' such that $Q \preceq Q''$
10:      Update $Q^??$ with the rules $Q' \preceq Q$
11:   **end if**
12:   **[New search space]** If the path reached the maximum depth, search on the nodes that are not linked to any verified node
13:   $B \leftarrow B - 1$
14: **end while**

Challenges and Future Directions: Data cleaning is of paramount interest to ensure the quality of data and reliable results on analyses tasks. Example-based approaches pave the way to intuitive interfaces and ensures data quality integrating user expertise. However, current solutions do not exploit examples and leave little freedom to the user choices. So far, the discovery process and the feedback is limited to query assessment [He et al., 2016] while more complex questions could be asked to the user.

Seemingly, there is no sharing of expertise or knowledge among tasks and datasets; if a user knows cleaned, or more accurate, data, such expertise should be transferred. This knowledge transfer is related to inductive transfer in machine learning [West et al., 2007].

2.5   EXAMPLE-BASED DATA EXPLORATION SYSTEMS

Some systems like Bleau [Sellam and Kersten, 2016a], Ziggy [Sellam and Kersten, 2016b], and QPlain [Deutch and Gilad, 2016a,b] have populated the research scene lately, showing the potential of example-based approaches in escorting the user toward the wanted answers. Such exploration tools have been introduced to assist the user in formulating queries with simple interfaces that assist the query formulation and understanding phase.

QPlain [Deutch and Gilad, 2016a,b] harnesses provenance models [Herschel et al., 2017] to generate additional explanations for the user. The considered provenance models are *conjunctive queries with inequalities*, which can be represented as *provenance polynomials* [Green, 2011]. In provenance polynomials, a query is treated as an expression with two operations: multiplication indicates joint tuples and summation indicates alternative derivations. For instance, to represent a journey from a place to another a table with starting and ending cities is expected to be joined multiple times to reach the final destination. Such *explanations* materialize different results that are proposed to the user, who is engaged in a search-and-refine process.

Bleau [Sellam and Kersten, 2016a] takes a clustering approach over the possible tuples, by partitioning the data along two dimensions. First, Bleau finds groups of mutually dependent attributes (columns) that represent a topic. An example of such groups in Figure 2.4 can be {bat,team} and {HR, stint}. Second, each group is partitioned internally using the attribute values (e.g., *HR* > 20) in a tree-shaped visualization. The resulting trees are then shown to the user who can navigate through complex portions of the dataset easily. An example of such tree-shaped visualization is shown in Figure 2.14.

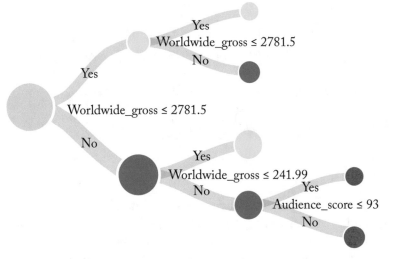

Figure 2.14: The Bleau interface.

Ziggy [Sellam and Kersten, 2016b] supports the user with statistics over a set of examples. Such examples are decomposed into views over groups of attributes in which the statistical distribution of the user's tuples is different from that of the rest of the data. The views are ranked using a *difference score* among the data and the examples and validated through conventional statistical tests, such as chi-square. Ziggy sustains high-dimensional data and needs little supervision from the user.

Trifacta [Chen, 2015] is a commercial interactive system for data cleaning. The system includes a proprietary example-based approach to define cleaning rules. Trifacta represents a notable case for reducing the effort of the user by employing simple and expressive examples.

Remark 2.16   Such visualizations are useful for navigating the data, but the use of examples is still limited to pure search-and-click approaches or complex explanations which are not directly controlled by the user.

Challenges and Future Directions: There is a consistent asymmetry between the evolution of data exploration practices and the actual data exploration systems. Although the advancements in query reverse engineering have paved a path toward systems requiring little or no user intervention through example-based approaches, no commercial system supports such semantics. Data visualization is a daunting task, especially because while the size of the screen to visualize the results does not scale linearly with the size of the datasets. Also, intuitive interfaces for exploration should focus on only the relevant information without overloading the user and without missing important insights. Therefore, the development of navigation interfaces should connect with other research communities, such as Human-Computer Interaction [Bhowmick et al., 2017].

On the other hand, the development of such systems requires a consistent work on the storage side, where data should be retrieved fast and reliably. The intersection between example-based methods, inherently vague and data exploration [Idreos et al., 2015] could lead to fruitful results.

Learning navigation models as in AIDE [Dimitriadou et al., 2014, 2016] could also help the exploration of such complex spaces. Such systems could also consider other tasks such as data cleaning and profiling [Naumann, 2014].

2.6   SUMMARY

This chapter sheds light on approaches where examples simplify complex exploratory tasks, such as reverse engineering queries (REQ) (Section 2.2), schema mapping (Section 2.3), or data cleaning (Section 2.4). The example-based approach eases the exploration process, since users employ objects they are familiar with. The exploration process becomes intuitive and expressive, as the user provides tuples, tables, or matching elements to perform the desired task. Recently, exploration system prototypes (Section 2.5) have demonstrated the practicality of example-based methods, and paved the road to commercial software and research tools. Figure 2.15 shows an overview of questions that example-based approaches can answer.

The exploration process starts with the object of the search, whether *tuples* or *matching rules*. The search for set of tuples leads to Reverse Engineering SQL (Section 2.2) queries which are automatically generated from the user's examples. Weiss and Cohen [2017] studies the hardness of the problem of finding the exact SQL query matching the example tuples.

Matching rules define logical predicates to integrate datasets having different schemas [Alexe et al., 2011a,b, Bonifati et al., 2016, Cate et al., 2013, Gottlob and Senellart, 2010] (Section 2.3), or to resolve entities [Singh, 2016] (Section 2.4.1) and perform data repair (Section 2.4.2).

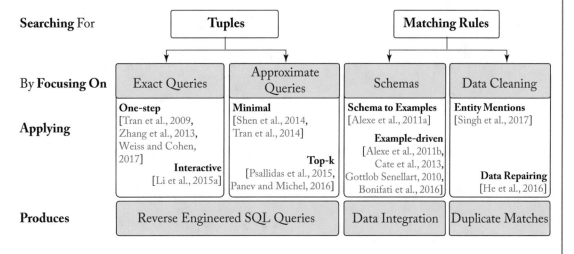

Figure 2.15: Overview of the techniques presented in this chapter.

CHAPTER 3

Graph Data

In this chapter, we survey techniques for identifying elements and structures of interest within a large graph.

Example 3.1   Recall the case of the sales manager. Brand X wants to advertise its services on a professional networking platform (e.g., LinkedIn). This platforms stores business information and relationships, such as who has worked where and with whom. Jodi should help the marketing department in identifying the characteristics of their target audience. It is not immediately clear how they can identify such users. What are the defining characteristics of their audience? How should the target audience look like? If they have a list of current customers, what if they could start the exploration from these users, and navigate the social network to identify other new customers? The target customers may belong to communities with common interests, or connections to current customers (Section 3.2), or they may have similar traits, connections to companies, relationships, and roles of the same type (either described by queries, Section 3.3, or similar complex structures, Section 3.4).

We start by defining the general model for graph data and its different declinations (Section 3.1). Then, we will discuss how to identify important nodes based on how they are connected with an initial set of seed nodes (Section 3.2). Such methods work for generic unlabeled undirected graphs, and for graphs that can have nodes annotated with a set of features or attributes. Then, moving to a richer model, we will discuss how to identify entities of interest in a knowledge graph. In this second case, the entity properties and entity types determine when two elements are similar, and this guides the retrieval of the entities related to a set provided as input. Finally, we will look into methods designed to retrieve complex structures. Similarly to what discussed in Chapter 2, the first set of techniques tries to reverse-engineer some form of graph-queries based on the user input and all the structures matching the query are then returned as answers (Section 3.3). The second set of techniques, instead, allows the user to provide a (possibly incomplete) specification of the structures of interest in the graph, i.e., a subgraph, and then the system identifies other subgraphs with the same structure (Section 3.4). When this is not possible, or it is time-consuming, only the top-k results will be produced.

Exploring Graphs: Graphs conveniently model data in several formats. The graph model is well suited to represent semi-structured data where the relationship between the data-items are as important and as rich as the items they connect. In this type of repositories, a great deal of information intertwines with the structure of the graph itself. For instance, in a citation network the connectivity between papers does not stop at the one-to-one relationship between the cited paper and citing one. Indeed, two papers cited by the same one are related as well. By navigating the citations, one can identify a cascade of influential papers. Similarly, an item in a graph is also defined by its connections, and by how other items influence it.

As a consequence of this, to query a graph we specify information about the items we are interested in, but also about the structure in which they are embedded. Yet, in a graph we are usually aware of some items (nodes) that we know to be similar to what we are looking for, but we are not sure about how the features that make them *relevant* translate to structures and connections. For instance, given a couple of documents, we would retrieve documents describing related issues, or given a couple of people from a target audience (e.g., customers in a social network) we may wish to identify people in the same community or with similar interests. Importantly, the requirement of different applications is likely very different.

Exploration methods for graph data allow the user to provide sample nodes or sample structures that act as the starting exploration point; the system then navigates the surrounding nodes to retrieve the answers. Therefore, the answers depend on how the system decides to steer such navigation.

3.1   THE GRAPH DATA MODEL

Graphs represent networks of objects (often called entities) linked one to another through relationships of different nature. Graphs are often chosen as models when it is important to focus both on the entities involved and on the connections among them.

There are different models for graphs (see Figure 3.1 for some examples). The simplest is the one of a tuple $G : \langle V, E, \phi \rangle$, where V is the set of vertices (also called nodes), E is the set of edges (which describe relationships among nodes), and ϕ is a function that assigns a unique identifier to each node $\phi: V \mapsto \mathbb{N}$. In practice, edges describe pairs of nodes $\langle v_1, v_2 \rangle$, where $v_1, v_2 \in V$, i.e., $E \subseteq V \times V$, and through ϕ we identify each single node, but no other information is stored about them or their connections. This model can represent only the structure of the network, i.e., its topology. All nodes and all the connections among them have the same semantics. The only distinction that may exist is whether the network is *directed* or *undirected*. In the latter case, the connection between two nodes is symmetric, i.e., $\langle v_1, v_2 \rangle \in E \rightarrow \langle v_2, v_1 \rangle \in E$. This is the case, for instance, of friendship relationships in a social network, where *Alex is friend-of Brook* also means that *Brook is friend-of Alex*. In the case of directed edges, for instance, links between web pages, where one page linking to another, is not necessarily reciprocal. The model of simple graphs (either directed or undirected) has been used in proximity and density based search methods,

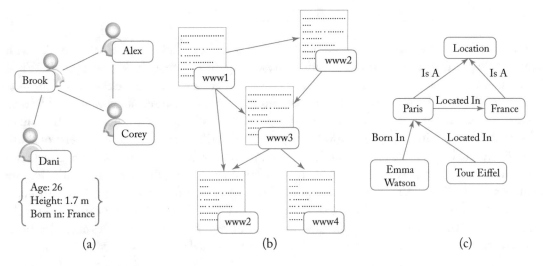

Figure 3.1: Three different types of graph data: (a) a friendship network (undirected unlabeled graph); (b) a web-graph (directed unlabeled graph); and (c) a knowledge graph (directed labeled graph). Nodes can also contain attributes as happens with the node of **Dani** in (a).

like those by Gionis et al. [2015, 2017], Kloumann and Kleinberg [2014], and Ruchansky et al. [2015].

Graphs can be used to represent richer information. For instance, one may enrich nodes with attributes (e.g., *domain*, *title*, and *creation date* for web pages), or they store information about node types (e.g., *person*, *photo*, and *post* in a social network). To store node attributes, we assume an alphabet of attribute names $\mathcal{N}$ and a set of values Ω. Each node has one or more attributes in the form of name-value pairs, by means of a function $\gamma : V \times \mathcal{N} \mapsto \Omega$, and we define an attributed graph as $G : \langle V, E, \phi, \mathcal{N}, \Omega, \gamma \rangle$, this is the model, for instance, studied in the case of focused clustering by Perozzi et al. [2014].

To store only node-types, instead, we assume an alphabet of labels $\mathcal{L}$, and a labeling function $\ell : V \mapsto \mathcal{L}$, and obtain a labeled graph $G : \langle V, E, \phi, \mathcal{L}, \ell \rangle$. Note that also edges can be labeled in the same way, i.e., by defining $\ell : E \mapsto \mathcal{L}$. In particular, for the case of directed edge-labeled graphs, there is, in practice, one-to-one correspondence with the model adopted by the Resource Description Framework specification (RDF) and its query language (SPARQL; see Arenas and Ugarte [2017]).

The objective of searching in edge labeled graphs is to find nodes connected by edges of specific types, as studied by Mottin et al. [2016] and Jayaram et al. [2015], or paths formed by a limited set of connections, which is the case of path queries [Bonifati et al., 2015]. For RDF, specifically, we will see how to study entity similarity [Metzger et al., 2013, Sobczak et al., 2015] and how to reverse engineer SPARQL queries [Arenas et al., 2016, Diaz et al., 2016].

3.2   SEARCH BY EXAMPLE NODES

One large family of search tasks on graphs have nodes as the object of the search. We start with the simple model of a network and consider unlabeled graphs (as those in Figures 3.1a,b). When searching for nodes, the user input is a set of nodes that are known to be relevant, and the output is a subset of the network that comprises both the nodes of interest, as well as additional nodes that are similarly related, or explain the connections among the former. We can think of a subset of people in a social network, where edges describe mutual-friendship relationships, and the desired output are members of the same community. Since we consider non-typed relationships, the only aspect that we can study to discriminate among them is how tightly they are connected (Section 3.2.1). For the case of attributed graphs, similarity among node attributes will be exploited to prioritize among connections (Section 3.2.2). For more expressive models, like those of RDF graphs (or in general of information graphs), node attributes and edge types help distinguish among entities that are involved in similar relationships (Section 3.2.3).

3.2.1   CONNECTIVITY AND CLOSENESS

The question we want to answer is: *Given a small set of query nodes Q, what specific region G' of the graph are they identifying?* Once we have identified such region, nodes within that region are the answer nodes. For instance, considering the green nodes in Figure 3.2, we could retrieve the community delimited by the dashed line as output.

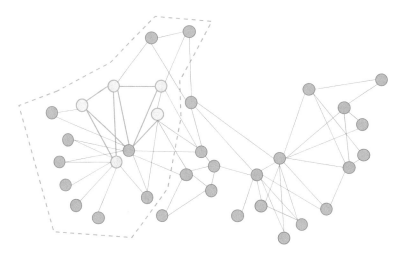

Figure 3.2: The seed expansion problem: given a set of seed nodes (colored) return all the other nodes that are closely related, for some relatedness definition (within dashed-line).

Seed Set Expansion

In Kloumann and Kleinberg [2014], the query nodes are also called *seed nodes*, and the answer nodes are members of the same cluster or community C. For this, the problem is referred to as *seed set expansion*.

Problem 3.2 Seed set expansion. Given a graph G, and a set of query nodes $V_Q \subseteq V_G$, retrieve all other nodes $V_C \subseteq V_G$, where C is a community in G, i.e., a connected subgraph of G, and $V_Q \subseteq V_C$.

In their study, they survey a number of methods for this task and evaluate their effectiveness and trade-offs. Each method accepts as input a small set of nodes V_Q and a large graph G and retrieves a subgraph C' of the graph G. Equipped with an indicator function that recognizes whether the node v belongs to some predefined community C, basically a ground-truth, and given a subset of nodes V_Q from C, $V_Q \subseteq V_C$, they compute the precision and recall for the retrieved set of nodes in $V_{C'}$.

Within a network, the intuitive definition of a community is a portion of the graph where nodes have many more connections inside the community than outside. As such, Kloumann and Kleinberg [2014] found that the most efficient algorithm to retrieve the members of a community given some seed members is based on the computation of a Personalized Page-Rank (for instance as in Jeh and Widom [2003]).

The result of a Personalized Page Rank computation is a vector $\mathbf{v}^t$, with size $|\mathbf{v}^t| = n$ the number of nodes in the graph, where the i-th value $\mathbf{v}_i^t \in [0, 1]$ represents the probability that a random walk starting in one of the seed nodes V_Q ends in node i at time t. To compute such vector, we consider the adjacency matrix $\mathbf{M}$, which is a square matrix of dimension n, where the position $\mathbf{M}_{i,j} = 1$ if and only if there exists in the graph a link between node i and node j and 0 otherwise. In this matrix, the degree of node i is given by $d_i = \sum_j \mathbf{M}_{i,j}$. The random walk vector is initialized at time $t = 0$ as $\mathbf{v}^0$, where $\mathbf{v}_i^0 = \frac{1}{|V_Q|}$ if $i \in V_Q$ and 0 otherwise. The final vector is computed iteratively. In particular, at each step $t + 1$, each node i distributes $\alpha \mathbf{v}_i^t$ probability mass uniformly over the initial query set V_Q (i.e., they restart), and $(1 - \alpha)\mathbf{v}_i^t$ over the neighbors nodes. Hence, we have the following:

$$\mathbf{v}^{t+1} = (1 - \alpha)\mathbf{M} \cdot \mathbf{v}^t + \alpha \mathbf{v}^0. \tag{3.1}$$

The result of the page rank computation estimates with which probability a random walker starting from any of the seed nodes will end on any other node in the graph. PPR technique effectively captures topological information about the network. In particular, if the walker is visiting a member of the community at time t, when transitioning at time $t + 1$ it will end more likely on another member of the same community.

Connector Nodes

Communities may be vast, and retrieving the complete list of all its members may be impractical. However, communities usually have a leader or a small set of central and influential figures. As such, the works of Tong and Faloutsos [2006], Gionis et al. [2015, 2017], and Ruchansky et al. [2015] address a different problem: given a set of seed nodes, retrieve a connected portion of the graph that explains in some way how the query nodes are connected. In this way, instead of retrieving all the members of a community, they retrieve a smaller subset of representative nodes. This concept has been applied, for instance, to identify hubs or influencers in a subnetwork, and to explain why nodes of a group are related one to the other.

Center-Piece Subgraph search. The first problem in this area is described by Tong and Faloutsos [2006] as the problem of *Center-Piece Subgraph search*, where, given a set of query nodes Q and a graph G, the task is to determine a set of nodes $V_{\mathcal{H}}$ that identifies a connected subgraph $\mathcal{H}$ which contains all (or almost all) the nodes in Q and for which the nodes maximize a *goodness* function $g(\mathcal{H})$. Therefore, depending on the definition of *goodness* employed, different sets of nodes will be retrieved. In particular, the problem definition in Tong and Faloutsos [2006] can be formalized as follows.

Problem 3.3 Center-Piece Subgraph Search (CEPS)   Given a set of query nodes V_Q, and a "goodness" function $g : V \mapsto \mathbb{R}^+$, find the best *connected* subgraph $\mathcal{H}^* = argmax_{\mathcal{H}} g(V_{\mathcal{H}})$.

The $g(V_{\mathcal{H}})$ is defined over each node $v_i \in V_{\mathcal{H}}$ and is based on the nodes in V_Q such that

$$g(V_{\mathcal{H}}) = \sum_{v_i \in V_{\mathcal{H}}} g(v_i) = \sum_{v_i \in V_{\mathcal{H}}} r(V_Q, v_i)$$

for some function r that provides a score for every single node. Hence, the goodness of each node in the answer is evaluated against the entire set of query nodes. To this end, they define the function $r(q_j, v_i)$, that is computed for a single query node $q_j \in V_Q$, so that $r(V_Q, v_i)$ is the result of the composition of $r(q_j, v_i)$ for all query nodes V_Q.

Furthermore, Tong and Faloutsos [2006] require the resulting graph to be connected, although they do not require for it to be fully connected. For instance, if we assume to be querying a co-citation network, we would like to find, given an initial set of authors, the set of other authors that have strong connections with all of (or most of) them. Through this process we would be able to identify mutual advisors, other members of the research group, or influential authors in the research area in which the authors in input publish the most (e.g., see in Figure 3.3). Depending on the input, we may be interested in nodes with strong connections to all of the input (the AND semantics), or we could require that the nodes retrieved are connected to at least k nodes from the input (see Figure 3.3), i.e., the *K_softAND* semantics (with $k \leq |V_Q|$).

The proposed solution to the Center-Piece Subgraph is threefold.

1. **Individual score calculation:** For each node $q_i \in V_Q$ and $v_j \in V_G$, compute $r(q_i, v_j)$.

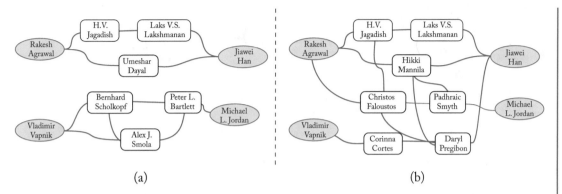

(a)   (b)

Figure 3.3: Answers to a Center Piece Subgraph query of 3 nodes (darker fill): (a) *K_softAND* semantics and (b) *AND* semantics (full connections).

2. **Individual score aggregation:** Combine all scores $r(q_i, v_j)$, for a given v_j, in order to obtain $r(V_Q, v_j)$.

3. **CEPS extraction:** Extract the connected subgraph $\mathcal{H}$ which maximizes $g(V_{\mathcal{H}})$, computed through each $r(V_Q, v_j)$ score.

Note that there is no implied limit enforced by the goodness function g in Problem 3.3. Yet, extracting the CEPS is hardly useful if the resulting graph $\mathcal{H}$ is large. For this reason, Tong and Faloutsos [2006] added an extra condition by introducing a budget b that limits the maximum size of nodes in $\mathcal{H}$, i.e., the extra condition requires that $|V_{\mathcal{H}}| \leq b$.

Finally, Tong and Faloutsos [2006] define the scoring function $r(q_i, v_j)$ and consequently $r(V_Q, v_j)$. Both scoring functions are computed by means of a random walk with restart starting respectively from the single node q_i or each node in V_Q. That is, the score $r(q_i, v_j)$ is the steady-state probability that a particle starting in q_i will end up in v_j, while $r(V_Q, v_j)$, is the steady-state probability that $n = |V_Q|$ particles starting each one on a node in V_Q will meet all on the node v_j.

For the case of the *K_softAND* formulation, $r(V_Q, v_j)$ is actually computed as the meeting probability of k particles, i.e., $r(V_Q, k, v_j)$. Hence, it describes the steady-state probability that at least k of V_Q particles of a random walk from the query nodes V_Q, will all find themselves at node v_j. Note that the computation for $r(V_Q, k, v_j)$ is a generalization of $r(V_Q, v_j)$. As a matter of fact, if we require the meeting probability for all nodes in V_Q, we can simply compute $r(V_Q, |V_Q|, v_j)$.

We can notice that the scores computed in Tong and Faloutsos [2006] are based on the result of a Personalized Page Rank computation, which, as a choice, is consistent with the result of Kloumann and Kleinberg [2014] seen above.

Algorithm 3.5 Center Piece Subgraph Extraction

Input: Query nodes V_Q, Graph G, max path length *len*, budget b, param. k
Output: Center Piece Subgraph $\mathcal{H}$

1:   $\mathcal{H} \leftarrow$ new Graph()
2:   **while** size($\mathcal{H}$) < b **do**
3:     $\bar{v} \leftarrow argmax_{v_i \in V_G \setminus V_{\mathcal{H}}}(r(V_Q, k, v_i))$
4:     **for each** $q_i \in V_Q$ **do**
5:       *toAdd* $\leftarrow$ new Path($q_i, \bar{v}$)
6:       merge(*toAdd*, $\mathcal{H}$)
7:     **end for**
8:   **end while**
9:   **return** $\mathcal{H}$

When all the scores have been computed, a dynamic programming algorithm will start from the query nodes and will try to connect those with other destination nodes based on their score. To this end, the algorithm will set a maximum allowed path length *len* and then will augment the answer graph with a new path between one of the query nodes and the graph node with the highest score (see Algorithm 3.5). This algorithm will effectively grow the target graph $\mathcal{H}$ until the desired budget b has been allocated.

The Wiener Connector. Among the approaches that, given a set of example nodes, retrieve a new set of nodes that try to explain the connection between them, a compelling solution is to find the *minimum Weiner connector*. This approach takes the name from the *Wiener index* (introduced by Wiener [1947]) which measures the *compactness* of a graph as the sum of all pairwise shortest-path distances between its vertices. The problem has been introduced by Ruchansky et al. [2015] and has been proven to be **NP**-hard. Its formulation is the following.

Problem 3.4 Minimum Wiener Connector   Given a set of query nodes V_Q, find the **connected** subgraph $\mathcal{H}^* = argmin_{\mathcal{H}} W_{idx}(\mathcal{H})$, where W_{idx} is the Wiener index of $\mathcal{H}$, which is computed as

$$\sum_{\{u,v\} \subseteq V_{\mathcal{H}}} d_{\mathcal{H}}(u, v),$$

where $d_{\mathcal{H}}(u, v)$ is the length of the shortest path between u and v within $\mathcal{H}$.

This approach tries to optimize the inter-node distance between each pair of members, and as a byproduct, this formulation has the desired effect to limit the size of the subgraph identified as a solution. Despite its hardness, Ruchansky et al. [2015] describe an effective approximation strategy that allows retrieving small and meaningful answers in reasonably short time. In contrast, other methods (like those seen above) either return very large subgraphs, since they reconstruct the entire community, or do not guarantee the solution to be fully connected, or tend to be slower because of the cost of the various random walks that have to be computed. Moreover, they usually require a user-defined budget for the size of the solution retrieved, while the Minimum Wiener Connector allows a parameter-free solution.

The problem of finding a small connected subgraph that brings together all the query nodes reminisce the Steiner Tree problem [Hwang et al., 1992]. However, Ruchansky et al. [2015] showed that Steiner Tree solutions provide no good solution to the Minimum Wiener problem. This is because the Steiner Tree may cause the solution to discard edges that are important to describe the centrality of some of the query nodes. As such, Ruchansky et al. [2015] provide a constant-factor approximation algorithm for the solution of the problem, and such solution is obtained by the summarization of the graph using multiple Steiner trees (see Algorithm 3.6).

Algorithm 3.6 Approximate Minimum Weiner Connector via Steiner Tree approximations

---

Input: Query nodes V_Q, Graph G, parameter $\beta > 0$
Output: Nodes of an Approximate Minimum Weiner Connector $\mathcal{H}$

1: $\forall v \in V_G, \forall q \in V_Q$ Compute $d_G(q, v)$
2: $\mathcal{H} \leftarrow \emptyset$
3: **for each** $t \in \left[1, \lceil log_{1+\beta}|V|\rceil\right]$ **do**
4:      $\lambda \leftarrow (1 + \beta)^t$
5:      **for each** $r \in V_Q$ **do**
6:          Get weighted graph $G_{r,\lambda} : \langle V_{r,\lambda}, E_{r,\lambda}\rangle$ rooted in r
7:          **for each** $e : (u, v) \in E_{r,\lambda}$ **do**
8:              $w(u, v) \leftarrow \lambda + \frac{max(d_G(r,u), d_G(r,v))}{\lambda}$
9:          **end for**
10:          $T \leftarrow$ ApproxSteinerTree$(G_{r,\lambda}, V_Q)$
11:          $\mathcal{H} \leftarrow \mathcal{H} \cup \langle T, r\rangle$
12:      **end for**
13: **end for**
14: **return** $argmin_{\langle T,r\rangle \in \mathcal{H}}$approxW$(T, r)$

In particular, in their solution, each query node is, in turn, considered as a candidate root node for a minimum-weight Steiner Tree. Weights on the edges of the tree are computed w.r.t. the distance between the chosen root and each other node. With this approximation strategy, the algorithm in Ruchansky et al. [2015] finds solutions that are quite near to the optimal in few minutes for graphs with millions of nodes. The actual approximation of the Weiner Index they optimize is computed as

$$\text{approxW}(T, r) = |V_T| \cdot \sum_{u \in V_T} d_T(u, r)$$

that is not suitable for online applications, but could be efficiently employed both for business analytics use-cases, or precomputed solutions for recommending systems.

Local discrepancy maximization. The idea of finding regions of the graph that explain the connections of some restricted set of query nodes V_Q is also studied by Gionis et al. [2015, 2017]. In particular, the problem presented in this work is called *local discrepancy maximization*, or "bump hunting," and describes the task of retrieving, given a set of query nodes that exhibit a certain property of interest, a connected subgraph where such nodes (or a subset) appear more often compared to non-query nodes.

Nevertheless, here the set of input nodes is assumed to be large, and the output should focus only on a smaller portion, where the input nodes are denser (the "bump"). Given its definition, the Local discrepancy maximization problem does not entirely adhere to the example-based query paradigm, since not all the input examples are part of the desired output. One feature that makes this work particularly relevant for graph-search, and in particular node-based search and exploration, is its ability to include in the output some additional nodes that were not part of the input and that are relevant because of their connection with the input. In this sense, the local discrepancy identifies the other nodes that are relevant to the information need subsumed by the user input, despite not being part of it. Moreover, the possibility to discard some of the input nodes can prove particularly useful for approximate-search.

The formal definition of the local discrepancy maximization problem requires the definition of the linear discrepancy of some subgraph C of G.

Problem 3.5   Linear Discrepancy Maximization   Given a set of query nodes V_Q, a parameter $\alpha \in \mathbb{R}^+$, and the linear discrepancy function $g(G')$ defined for any subgraph G' of G as $g(G)= \alpha \cdot |V_Q \cap V_G| - |V_G \setminus V_Q|$, find the subgraph $\mathcal{H}^* = argmax_{\mathcal{H}}(g(\mathcal{H}))$.

The linear discrepancy maximization problem is proven to be **NP**-hard, but Gionis et al. [2015] demonstrate that when the input graph is a tree, the solution takes linear $O(|G|)$ time. For the general case, their approach is heuristic, and they solve the problem by reducing the graph to a tree (they study various alternatives for this step), producing in this way a reduced input graph, and then applying the linear-time algorithm on such restricted search space. However, those solutions all require multiple scans of the entire graph, which is initially assumed to reside into main memory completely.

Since such solution may be too costly for very large graphs, a local-access model is proposed. For the cases where the entire graph G is not entirely stored in memory, they study a *local-access model*. In such a model, the graph is not fully accessible as input. Instead, only the query nodes V_Q are given, while the rest of the graph can be accessed through a *neighbor function*. This function takes as input a single node and, by querying the graph, obtains the list of all other adjacent nodes.

In these settings, the key element for an efficient solution is to invoke the neighbor function only a limited number of times. To this end, in Gionis et al. [2015], three different strategies are studied, all with a common element: to iteratively build a smaller subgraph G' of G by expanding the query nodes (or only some of those) in V_Q and deciding then when to stop expanding. The stopping criterion is based on the number of query nodes, the size of the currently loaded graph G', and the distance between the candidate node to expand and the nearest query node. Of the three expansion techniques studied, two have a fixed stopping criterion, while the third (and most effective in general) implements an adaptive expansion strategy based on an upper-bound of the optimal solution scores. An important outcome of the experimental evaluation is that, for sparse graphs, even a fixed stopping criterion performs exceptionally well both in terms of running time and quality of the output.

3.2.2   CLUSTERS AND NODE ATTRIBUTES

Up to this point, we have considered problems that retrieve nodes whose relevance is based on their connectivity and respective closeness. In some cases, the above algorithms may take into consideration also edge-weights as a predefined and static (hence, not query-dependent) information about the strength or cost of the edges. Yet, all these solutions retrieve nodes considering only the topology of the graph.

Focused clustering. Many real-world graphs are provided with richer information in the form of node attributes. Consider, for instance, a social network (e.g., Figure 3.1a) where nodes are people connected by friendship relationships, and for each person, the network stores a profile as a set of node-attributes (e.g., name, demographics, or preferences). In this model, node-attributes are represented as *feature-vectors*, and while the user input is still a set of query nodes V_Q as in the previous problems, the query nodes provide an additional information carried by the values of the feature vectors of the query nodes themselves (see Figure 3.4).

The solution presented by Perozzi et al. [2014] is to infer attribute weights, which represent an implicit measure of the user preference toward some of the node attributes. Equipped with this information, they consider that, when considering the connectivity among nodes, not all connections have the same importance or strength. In this settings, the problem proposed is called *Focused clustering*, and is formalized as follows.

Problem 3.6   Focused Clustering   Given a graph G, where each node is associated with $n = |\mathcal{F}|$ features (also called node attributes), and a set of query nodes $V_Q \subseteq V_G$, infer a set of feature weights $\omega_F : \mathcal{F} \mapsto \mathbb{R}^+$, and extract a set of *focused cluster* $\mathcal{C}$, where each cluster C has nodes V_C that are (1) dense in graph structure and (2) coherent with the attributes with highest weights ω_F.

Furthermore, as a result of comparing members in each cluster, Perozzi et al. [2014] solve a second complementary problem: *focused outlier detection*, i.e., they identify in each cluster those nodes that deviate from the other nodes in the same cluster for some of their attribute values.

The approach followed by Perozzi et al. [2014] to find both clusters and outliers is composed by three steps.

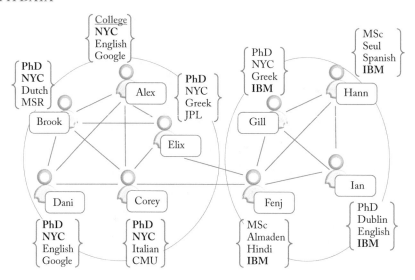

Figure 3.4: Example graph with two focused clusters and one focused outlier (based on Perozzi et al. [2014]).

1. **Attribute weights inference:** This translates to an instantiation of the distance learning problem [Xing et al., 2003], where the goal is to find an appropriate distance function for computing the distance between two feature vectors f_i, f_j, for nodes $v_i, v_j \in V$, such that given two nodes their distance is smaller if they both are in the same cluster C that if one of the two laid outside it. The distance function is modeled as $(f_i - f_j)^T \mathbf{A}(f_i - f_j)$, and the nature of the distance function depends thus on $\mathbf{A}$. For instance, setting $\mathbf{A}$ as the identity matrix corresponds to calculating the Euclidean distance. In their work, Perozzi et al. [2014] propose learning the values for $\mathbf{A}$ based on the attribute values of the input nodes. In particular, they generate a set of positive pairs of nodes from the examples P_S : $\{(u, v) | u \in V_Q \wedge v \in V_Q\}$, and a set of negative pairs from nodes not chosen from the examples P_D : $\{(u, v) | u \notin V_Q \wedge v \notin V_Q\}$. These are then used to optimize the following objective function:

$$\min_A \sum_{(u,v)\in P_S} (f_i - f_j)^T \mathbf{A}(f_i - f_j) - \gamma log \left(\sqrt{(f_i - f_j)^T \mathbf{A}(f_i - f_j)} \right).$$

In optimizing the function, the learned matrix $\mathbf{A}$ is kept diagonal, this allows to assign one single score to each feature $\mathcal{F}$. The outcome of this step is the weighting function ω_F.

2. **Focused clusters extraction:** This step extracts clusters of nodes with high connectivity and also high feature-value coherence, i.e., those that form a community of nodes with almost the same value for those attributes with high weight in ω_F. The edges in the graph

are re-weighted according to the scores of ω_F, and only connected components with high-score weights are kept. These are the cores of the final set of clusters, with an iterative process those cores are then progressively expanded. During expansion, the weighted conductance (Andersen et al. [2006]) of each cluster is computed. That is, the algorithm measures the ratio between the weighted sum of edges crossing the boundaries of the cluster and the wighted sum of those residing within it. The expansion proceeds until no further improvement can be gained.

3. **Outlier detection:** In this process outliers are retrieved while computing clusters. In particular, outliers are those nodes that have a high un-weighted conductance, but a low weighted conductance.

We can see here a recurrent pattern employed to retrieve good solution in reasonable time, i.e., to iteratively expand around the query nodes, with the goal of avoiding complete scans of the whole graph.

3.2.3 SIMILAR ENTITY SEARCH IN INFORMATION GRAPHS

In the previous section, we described the idea of *focused clustering*, where the discovery of answer nodes was guided not only by their connectivity, but also by their attributes.

In this section, this same intuition is considered in a different form for the task of entity search for knowledge graphs, as studied by Metzger et al. [2013] and Sobczak et al. [2015]. As mentioned earlier, knowledge graphs are special directed edge-labeled graphs, where information about entities and concepts is represented as subject-predicate-object triples (as in the RDF data model). In this data model, a node in the graph can represent real-world entities, like a person, a place or an abstract concept, e.g., *Emma Watson* or *Paris* (see Figure 3.1c). Additional information is represented as edges between nodes. In this way, for each triple, the nodes represent subjects and objects, while predicates are translated to edge labels. These structures are part of the so-called *Fact Graph*. Furthermore, within the same graph, ontological information is also stored as an *Ontology Tree*, e.g., *Emma Watson* **is an** *Actor* and an *Actor* **is an** *Artist*. Within a knowledge graph, given an entity e, e.g., *Emma Watson*, all the facts that are connected to it, i.e., both edges in the fact graph or in the ontology tree, are called its aspects $A(e)$.

In this context, the works by Metzger et al. [2013] first and Sobczak et al. [2015] later describe the problem of *query by entity examples*, also called *aspect-based entity retrieval*, which can be formalized as follows.

Problem 3.7 Aspect-Based Entity Retrieval Given a knowledge graph G, and a set of query entities V_Q, retrieve a set of k entities V_C, with $|V_C| = k$, that are similar, i.e., share some aspects with the entities in V_Q, meaning that $A(V_Q) \cap A(V_C) \neq \emptyset$.

In the formulation of Metzger et al. [2013], the problem is to identify a set of aspects $A' \subseteq A(V_Q) = \bigcap_{v \in V_Q} A(v)^1$ that are common to all entities in the query, and that can retrieve new entities that are not present in it. In the graph terminology, the aspects of an entity are all the edges incident to it. In their work, Metzger et al. [2013] also distinguish the set of *basic aspects*, which are the type of edges that are incident to the entity. For instance, **was born in** *Paris* is an aspect, while **being born** (with no reference to the place) is a basic aspect. Moreover, through each aspect a they identify the set of entities that share that same aspect ($\mathcal{E}(a) \subseteq V_G$), called the entity set of a, e.g., the set of all the entities that are incident to an edge for **was born in** *Paris*.

Intuitively, some of the entities in the query will have certain aspects that are not shared by some other user-provided entities. Such aspects that are not shared by *all* user-provided entities are assumed to be not relevant for the user. Thus, we will need to consider only aspects that are common to all the entities. At the same time, if we keep *all* the aspects that are common to *all* the entities in the query, we could end up considering a set of aspects which is too restrictive and will not identify any other entity except those already provided. Hence, the solution designed by Metzger et al. [2013] is to retrieve a set of aspect $A' \subseteq A(V_Q)$ which contains as many aspects as possible, and, at the same time, which includes at least one entity that is not in V_Q, this is called a *maximal aspect set*. More formally, a maximal aspect set A^* of V_Q is defined as satisfying the following two conditions:

1. $A^* \subseteq A(V_Q)$, where $\bigcap_{a \in A^*} \mathcal{E}(a) \setminus V_Q \neq \emptyset$ and

2. $\forall a \in A(V_Q) \setminus A^*. \mathcal{E}(\{a\} \cup A^*) \setminus V_Q = \emptyset$, where $\mathcal{E}(A) = \bigcap_{a \in A} \mathcal{E}(a)$.

To retrieve such maximal aspects, they first retrieve the set of *basic aspects*, e.g., **was born in**. Then they consider for each basic aspect, those that have values shared by all the other entities, e.g., **was born in** *Paris*. A particular role is given to aspects related with the ontology tree, i.e., the types. They enforce each set of maximal aspects to contain at least one type, and among all the types, they give priority to those that are more specific, i.e., those that are lower in the in the ontology tree (e.g., actor instead of artist).

For a group of entities, there are usually multiple disjoint sets of aspects that satisfy the maximal condition. Hence, it is crucial to discriminate among the possible alternatives. To this end, in Metzger et al. [2013], they also perform a task called *aspect ranking*, where each aspect is assigned a score based on its selectivity (i.e., how frequent or infrequent it is in the knowledge graph), and based on some popularity score of the entities involved.

Their approach is implemented in the QBEES framework (see Algorithm 3.7), and later extended in the iQbees framework [Sobczak et al., 2015]. In their extension, they enable an interactive query mechanism. In practice, the user can provide an initial query set, and later

---

[1]Note that it is not guaranteed that $A(V_Q) \neq \emptyset$, even though in general two entities share very generic aspects like *being an object*, *having weight*, and so on.

Algorithm 3.7 Entity-List Completion

Input: Query nodes V_Q, Graph G, parameter k
Output: Entity Set **E**
 1: $\mathbf{E} \leftarrow \emptyset$
 2: **while** $|\mathbf{E}| < k$ **do**
 3:     $\mathcal{M}_\mathcal{A} \leftarrow$ extractAspects($V_Q \cup \mathbf{E}$)
 4:     $A \leftarrow$ top($\mathcal{M}_\mathcal{A}$)
 5:     $e \leftarrow argmax_{e \in \mathcal{E}(A)} pop(e)$
 6:     $\mathbf{E} \leftarrow \mathbf{E} \cup \{e\}$
 7: **end while**
 8: **return E**

 9: **function** extractAspects($\bar{V}$)
10: **do**
11:     $\mathcal{A} \leftarrow \bigcap_{q \in \bar{V}} A(q)$
12:     $\mathcal{M}_\mathcal{A} \leftarrow$ maximalAspects($\bar{V}, \mathcal{A}, G$)
13:     $\mathcal{T} \leftarrow$ typicalTypes($\bar{V}$)
14:     $\mathcal{M}_\mathcal{A} \leftarrow \{A \in \mathcal{M}_\mathcal{A} | A \cap \mathcal{T} \neq \emptyset\}$
15:     rank($\mathcal{M}_\mathcal{A}$)
16: **return** $\mathcal{M}_\mathcal{A}$

---

refine it by adding additional entities, so that the set of maximal aspects is refined at every interaction.

A similar problem is also taken into consideration by Han et al. [2016], although with a specific focus on graph-pattern queries. Such work is not covered here, but in a sense, it can be seen as a more graph-centric implementation of the works described above.

Challenges and Future Directions: A large corpus of works has studied how to identify a cluster (a community) of nodes given some of its members. At their core, all these methods assume that the input and output nodes share the same node and edge types. Yet, in works like the one by Perozzi et al. [2014], node attributes play a major role and help distinguish relationships of different importance. **In heterogeneous information networks, e.g., knowledge graphs, the need to distinguish nodes and relationship types, and to infer the user preferences about them is at the forefront.** Hence, approaches similar to those employed for *focused clustering* need to be studied for edge-labeled graphs and extended to other tasks.

Moreover, exploratory search needs usually require interactivity. Yet, the only approach that allows for an interactive search work-flow has been studied for the task of entity search (iQbees, Sobczak et al. [2015]). **Therefore, interactive and personalized clustering and community detection systems are a natural extension for these works.**

3.3   REVERSE ENGINEERING QUERIES ON GRAPHS

Up to this point, we focused on finding nodes that are similar to those users provided as examples. In what follows, instead, we move our attention to specific sub-structures of the graph. In particular, similarly to what seen in Chapter 2, we will see how we can reverse-engineer specific types of graph-queries, namely: path queries and SPARQL queries.

3.3.1   LEARNING PATH QUERIES ON GRAPHS

The first work we consider treats the user need as a *path query* [Bonifati et al., 2015]. Path queries are described by regular expressions on edge labels. A path query defines all the paths that are allowed to be traversed in the graph. Consider for example the query (child_of|married_with)*+acted_in.[2] This query accepts paths in the graph that connect actors to movies, as well as people related to actors (in our example children or spouses). These queries are flexible and widely applicable; for instance, see Barceló Baeza [2013] and Wood [2012]. Yet, they are not so easy to be expressed by a novice user, or by somebody that is not aware of the structure of the knowledge graph. To overcome this limitation, Bonifati et al. [2015] embrace the exemplar paradigm. In particular, they allow the user to express their need by presenting some nodes in the form of positive and negative examples. In practice, continuing with our example, the user may provide a set of actors or people related to actors alongside some movies as positive examples, while it might present some singers and songs as examples of entities that are not of interest.

The task is then to derive a path query that generates paths that (i) are covered by all the positive examples and (ii) do not cover any of the negative ones. Although the previous example presents a case where the query specifies both starting and ending nodes, in Bonifati et al. [2015], the problem studied is even more generic and allows the user to specify just one end of the path of interest, e.g., the starting or the ending node. In this formulation, this approach can also be used for similarity entity search, as described in the previous section, but for cases in which simple aspects are not sufficient to describe why the entities are relevant.

As mentioned earlier, path queries are based on the concept of regular expressions.

Definition 3.8 Regular expressions.   A regular language is defined by a regular expression generated by the following grammar:

$$q := \epsilon \,|\, a(a \in \Sigma) \,|\, q_1 + q_2 \,|\, q_1 \cdot q_2 \,|\, q^*,$$

---

[2]The symbol | is the disjunction, ∗ is the equivalent of the Kleene star, and + is the concatenation symbol.

where Σ is the alphabet of edge labels, "$\cdot$" denotes concatenation, "$+$" denotes disjunction, and "$*$" denotes the Kleene star.

Given a query q, $L(q)$ denotes the language generated by it. For example, the query $(a|b)^* \cdot c$ will generate a language containing words like c, ac, $aabc$, and so on.

A path is obtained from a sequence of edges by considering the edge-labels encountered. For instance, given the subgraph represented by *Emma Watson* **born in** *Paris* **located in** *France*, we obtain the path expression **born in** $\cdot$ **located in**. A path p matches a path query q, if p is member of the language $L(q)$. Then, given a node $v \in V_G$ we identify all the paths that originate from it with *paths(v)*. The algorithm proposed by Bonifati et al. [2015] generates paths with a directed traversal of the graph starting from the designated node. Note that, if a directed loop is encountered, this algorithm generates an infinite series of paths. Hence the result is that the set *paths(v)* is an infinite set.

Given the definition above, the answer to a path query q on the graph G is then the set of nodes which are source of at least one path that is member of the language generated by the query, i.e., $q(G) = \{v \in G | L(q) \cap paths(v) \neq \emptyset\}$. As we mentioned, in the work of Bonifati et al. [2015], the user is providing two sets of examples: positive and negative examples. Hence, the problem they solve is the following.

Problem 3.9 Learning Path Queries   Given a set of positive examples $S^+ \subseteq V_G$ and a set of negative example $S^- \subseteq V_G$, with $S^+ \cap S^- = \emptyset$, retrieve the set of queries Q, such that $q \in Q \Rightarrow S^+ \subseteq q(G) \wedge S^- \cap q(G) = \emptyset$.

In general, the problem defined by Bonifati et al. [2015] indicates the pair made with the set of positive and negative examples as the *sample* $S : \langle S^+, S^- \rangle$ for the query. A sample (a set of positive and negative examples) is *consistent* when it does not contradict itself, and as such it allows for a solution to exist. Hence, the first problem is to determine whether a generic input sample is consistent. They demonstrate that, in general, the problem is **PSPACE**-complete. Given this result, they provide both a characterization of what class of queries is learnable and the proof that the problem of learning generic graph pattern queries is **NP**-complete.

To overcome this complexity, they characterize a class of queries which is *learnable with abstain*. Namely, they describe a learning algorithm (Algorithm 3.8) that, always in polynomial time, returns either a query consistent with the sample or a special *null* value that indicates either that not enough examples are provided to return an answer or that such query does not exists. In particular, the algorithm provides both the following guarantees.

1. **Soundess with Abstain:** For every graph G, and sample $S : \{S^+, S^-\}$, the algorithm returns either a query in $q \in Q$ that is consistent with the examples, or null if no such query exists or it cannot be constructed efficiently.

2. **Completeness:** For every query q there exists a polynomially-sized characteristic sample $CS : \{S_{CS}^+, S_{CS}^-\}$ on G, s.t. for every other sample $\bar{S}$ extending CS consistently with q (i.e., $S_{CS}^+ \subseteq \bar{S}^+, S_{CS}^- \subseteq \bar{S}^-$) the algorithm on input G and $\bar{S}$ returns q.

These guarantees allow the algorithm to either return the correct answer very quickly or to give to the user the possibility to extend the initial sample when the provided input is not sufficient to identify the correct answer efficiently, enabling in this way an interactive query-discovery process.

To obtain answers in polynomial time, they fix a maximum path length k, which can be chosen offline according to the structure of the graph and on the application. Given the maximum length k, the algorithm enumerates all paths originated from the positive examples S^+ and subtracts from such set all those that are generated by the negative samples S^-. The paths obtained in this step are called *smallest consistent paths* (SCP). Yet, those use only disjunction and concatenation. To exploit the full expressibility of the language, a *generalization step* is performed. This step compacts queries and introduces the use of the Kleene star. This process builds first a Prefix-Tree Acceptor (PTA) [De la Higuera, 2010] for the language generated by the SCP, then it compacts it into a Deterministic Finite-state Automaton (DFA) (see Figure 3.5).

Algorithm 3.8 Learning Path Queries

Input: Sample $S : \{S^+, S^-\}$, Graph G, max length k
Output: Path query q or *null*

1: $P \leftarrow \emptyset$
2: **for each** $v \in S^+$ **do**
3: $P \leftarrow P \cup \{min_\leq(paths_G^k(v) \backslash paths_G^k(S^-))\}$
4: **end for**
5: $A \leftarrow$ prefixTreeAcceptor(P)
6: **while** $\exists s, s' \in A$ s.t. $L(A_{s \mapsto s'}) \cap paths_G^k(S^-) = \emptyset$ **do**
7: $A \leftarrow A_{s \mapsto s'}$
8: **end while**
9: **if** $\forall v \in S^+. L(A) \cap paths_G^k(v) \neq \emptyset$ **then**
10:   **return** computeDFA(A)
11: **end if**
12: **return** *null*

The process is demonstrated to generate queries that satisfy the user need. Moreover, as a result of the completeness property of the algorithm by Bonifati et al. [2015], the framework allows for an interactive query-learning process. In particular, they describe an active process, where the system poses to the users a question regarding specific nodes to be labeled as positive or negative examples. The challenge is then in minimizing the number of nodes to present to

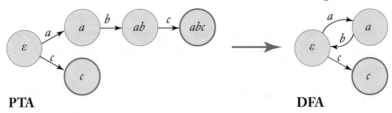

PTA   **DFA**

Figure 3.5: PTA (left) and DFA (right) obtained for the language $(a \cdot b)^* \cdot c$ (based on Bonifati et al. [2015]).

the user for labeling. The solution they devise identifies a set of nodes as *informative*, i.e., nodes that generate at least one path that is not generated by any node among the negative examples.

3.3.2   REVERSE ENGINEERING SPARQL QUERIES

The last work we will cover regards the SPARQL query language (see Gallego et al. [2011] and Pérez et al. [2009]). SPARQL is specifically designed as web standard by the W3C (World Wide Web Consortium)[3] for RDF datasets. Informally, given an RDF dataset as a set of RDF subject-predicate-object (s-p-o) triples, a SPARQL query has the form of a template matching query, which is composed by s-p-o triples itself, but where some subject, objects or predicates are replaced by variables. Triples in a SPARQL query may be joined by **AND** conjunctions, or enriched by **FILTER** statements where conditions are posed on top of the variables defined in some of the triples. For instance, the query that selects actors *born in Paris*, which *acted in* some movie is (?X, born_in, ``Paris'') **AND** (?X, acted_in ,?Y), with ?X and ?Y as symbols for variables. A filter condition could be of the form (?X,age,?A) FILTER ?A>18.

Answers to such queries are all the variable assignments that are satisfied in the dataset by some set of triples. The SPARQL query language also adopts an additional **OPT** operator, which retrieves a triple if it exists, but is not mandatory for an answer to be able to satisfy such condition. For instance, we could try to retrieve also the child of an actor by rewriting the query above as (?X born_in ``Paris'') **AND** (?X acted_in ?Y) **OPT** (?X has_child ?W). The result set of this last query is a superset of the previous query since we will retrieve all the possible actors born in Paris with their movie, but we will also retrieve their children, for those that have some, and without excluding those that do not have any.

The SPARQL query language is the language of choice for semantic web applications [Gallego et al., 2011], but despite its widespread use, it still poses a critical challenge to write SPARQL queries for users that are unfamiliar with it or with the graph they are querying. To provide a more effective way to formulate SPARQL queries, Arenas et al. [2016] and Diaz et al. [2016] propose an approach that is similar in spirit to the original Query-by-Example

[3]https://www.w3.org/TR/2004/REC-rdf-primer-20040210/

paradigm of Zloof [1975]. Namely, given a set of example mappings, the system will retrieve one or more SPARQL queries that produce such mappings as subsets of their answer.

In particular, in the *SPARQLbyE* system, the user is asked to provide only a set of candidate variable mappings, e.g.,

- *e*1 :?X↦"Emma Watson," ?Y↦ "Paris," and

- *e*2 :?X↦"Jim Carrey."

Here, a mapping μ is a set of pairings between variables and values $\mu : \{(?X_1 \mapsto val_1), \ldots, (?X_n \mapsto val_n)\}$, and $dom(\mu)$ is the set of variables, i.e., $dom(\mu):\{?\lambda|(?\lambda\mapsto val) \in \mu\}$. Moreover, the user can avoid the specification of mapping for some of the variables in some of the examples, e.g., skipping the place of birth for "Jim Carrey" if they do not know it. In this way, the user can provide partial examples or **OPT** statements (see Figure 3.6).

	?X	?Y	?W	?Z
e1	Emma Watson	Paris	Harry Potter	
e2	Jim Carrey		The Truman Show	
e3	Will Smith			Jaden Smith

$$\downarrow$$

MATCH (?X, born_in, ?Y)
AND (?X, ̄acted_in, ?W)
OPT (?X, has_child, ?Z)

Figure 3.6: Reverse engineering SPARQL query from example matchings.

The task of reverse engineering SPARQL queries is in general computationally hard, although there are some exceptions, depending on whether we allow the full set of language constructs, and depending on what kind of examples we accept as input. In particular, Arenas et al. [2016] study three different problem instantiations, namely, the case in which the user provides only the positive examples, the case where the user also provides negative examples (similar to Bonifati et al. [2015]), and finally the case in which the query should return only the example mappings, and no other triple. Moreover, they also study the simpler problem of verifying whether a specific query satisfies a specific input.

Arenas et al. [2016] prove that both the verification and the reverse engineering task are solvable in polynomial time only for queries that use the **AND** operator and nothing else. A polynomial time solution exists if the use of the **OPT** operator is limited and if the mappings provided present some property called *tree*-like. This property holds when the sets of examples that map each variable can be arranged in a tree-shaped lattice under inclusion (see Figure 3.7). That is, given a set of mappings $\Omega : \{\mu_1, ..., \mu_k\}$, for each variable $?\lambda \in \Lambda : \{?P|\exists\mu \in \Omega, val.(?P \mapsto val) \in \mu\}$ instantiated by any mapping in Ω, we build the set of covered mapping

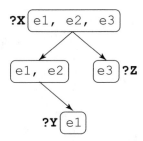

Figure 3.7: The set-inclusion lattice for the variable mappings in Figure 3.6.

$C(?\lambda)$:$\{\mu \in \Omega | \exists val.(?\lambda \mapsto val) \in \mu\}$. Then we organize each $?\lambda \in \Lambda$ in a lattice according to the relation $\subseteq$ (Figures 3.7 and 3.8). The lattice is then arbitrarily converted to a tree; such tree dictates the structure of the query. A greedy algorithm starts from the root of the tree, and then detects (by searching within the database) the set of predicates that satisfy its variable-value mappings. From each predicate a candidate query can be constructed, that is the core of the query. The set is then enriched with **OPT** by applying recursively the same approach by navigating toward the leaves of the three (see Figure 3.8).

These results are then exploited to build a system that can work on top of existing SPARQL endpoints and allow for this solution to work in practice for everyday web use [Diaz et al., 2016].

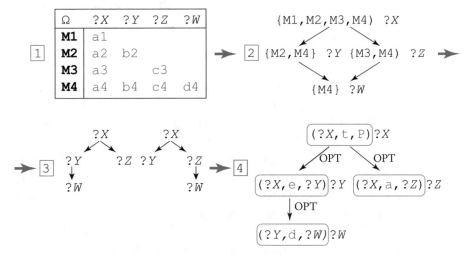

Figure 3.8: Overview of the reverse engineering process.

Challenges and Future Directions: As discussed in the chapter on the relational model (Chapter 2) and illustrated once more here, query reverse-engineering is a computationally expensive task in general. Nonetheless, the approaches presented above provide viable solutions to this problem in some situations. Yet, some questions of practical importance remain open. **The first concern is about scalability:** knowledge graphs and ontologies are sizable and contain thousands of relationship types, how do these systems behave in such conditions? The good news is that usually the search space of these methods can be bounded locally to the neighborhood of the provided examples, i.e., we do not necessarily need to scan the entire graph to interpret the user need. **Hence, appropriate index techniques could be studied to bootstrap these algorithms**.

On a different note, the approaches presented allow for interactivity in the discovery process, *but do not include the user-preference explicitly*. **Still, for the cases in which vague examples lead to a large number of candidate queries, it is important to study how to provide personalized rankings and query reformulation techniques.**

3.4   SEARCH BY EXAMPLE STRUCTURES

In this last section of the chapter, we survey methods that take into consideration general subgraph structures of the graph both as input and output. These methods resemble in some way the case of reverse engineering SPARQL queries but refer to more generic graph search via graph-homomorphism queries. In particular, we approach those cases in which the user-need translates to one or more sample *structures* that are considered relevant, and the system performs the necessary computations to retrieve all other substructures in the graph that match the input.

3.4.1   GRAPH QUERY VIA ENTITY-TUPLES

The first of these works is called **GQBE:** "Graph Query by Example" as proposed by Jayaram et al. [2015], and which is specifically designed for the case of knowledge graph search. The method reminisces Query by Example [Zloof, 1975], and its formulation is very similar to the previous method for reverse engineering SPARQL queries [Arenas et al., 2016]. The user provides one or more *entity tuples*, where each entity tuple is an ordered list of entities in the graph, e.g., ⟨*Jerry Yang, Yahoo!*⟩. The output is then a set of entity tuples that subsume the same structure, in this case, founders and the respective company.

There are two challenges that need to be addressed. The first is to identify which graph structures need to be taken in consideration, or in other words, what paths connect the entities in the tuple, and what other additional nodes not mentioned in the tuple should be taken in consideration. In some sense, there is a need to understand what additional aspects are relevant to the user (as it was happening in Metzger et al. [2013]). The second task is to retrieve from the graph all other entities that take part in the same type of connections, i.e., to perform a subgraph-isomorphism search (see Figure 3.9).

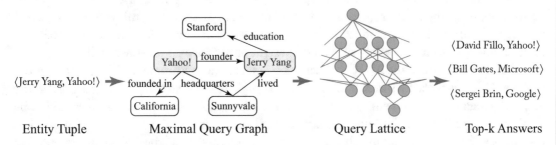

Figure 3.9: Graph Query by Entity-tuple: query processing overview.

To understand the information-need behind the entity-tuple provided by the user, Jayaram et al. [2015] propose the concept of *Query Graph*, which is a weakly connected subgraph of the knowledge graph that (1) contains all the nodes in the entity tuple and (2) contains at most m edges. In this case, m is a user-provided parameter that limits the size of the query graph, so to avoid it to be the entire knowledge graph, for instance.

Then, the query graph obtained in this way can explain how the query entities relate one to the other. In the example above, the query graph will need to contain the edge describing that *Jerry Yang* is **founder of** *Yahoo!*, but it may also include the fact *Yahoo!* was **founded in** *California*, which further limits the result-set.

By this formulation, multiple query graphs may exist. Consequently, in Jayaram et al. [2015], they first introduce the concept of *Maximal* Query Graph (MQG). The MQG is obtained by weighing the edges and maximizing the sum of the edge weights. This definition is still problematic since in practice finding such maximal graph is computationally intractable. Hence, a series of relaxations and heuristics are applied. In the end, the final MQG is built via a heuristic approach that runs several depth-first visits from each query entity and keeps only the top weighted edges.

Weights are also assigned based on a mixture of scoring formulas that take into consideration the popularity of the edge label, both globally in the entire knowledge graph, and also locally around each query entity.

Last but not least, answers should be isomorphic-subgraphs of the final MQG obtained in the previous step. Yet, such MQG may be too selective (i.e., its structure may be too complicated), and as such only few substructures in the graph may be found matching it. For this reason, in GQBE, a set of approximate answers are retrieved by generating a lattice of "simpler" query graphs.

In the lattice, the top node is the MQG itself, while all its children at the lower level are obtained by removing one-by-one its edges, but ensuring that all the query nodes are still present an that the graph is weakly connected.

The lattice is crucial for the top-k processing of the query. Query-Answers are ranked based on the edge weights in the query graph, and based on the nodes they share with the entities in the query. When it is time for graph-query-processing then, the lattice is explored bottom-up, from the simpler queries up to the more complex. During this exploration, some nodes in the lattice will be pruned either because already covered by some other nodes, or because their total weight cannot possibly surpass the weight of the answers already found.

Another feature of the MQG computation is that it can accommodate for multiple entity tuples as input, as far as they match the same entity tuple template. In this way, a maximal query graph is generated for each entity tuple, and then those graphs are aligned and merged in one single query graph before building the lattice. In this way, it is easier for the system to guess the edges and structures that match the user need. The overview of the process is presented in Figure 3.9.

3.4.2   QUERIES WITH EXAMPLE SUBGRAPHS

We now proceed to explain the last family of techniques that allow performing search on graphs via examples. This technique is called *exemplar queries* and has been introduced by Mottin et al. [2014]. The exemplar query paradigm, as with the other methods presented here, accepts as input an example member of the answer set. The query engine is then inferring the full answer set based on the example and any additional information provided by the underlying database. The answers are all those elements in the database that satisfy a predefined *congruence relation*.

Exemplar queries on graphs. The work by Mottin et al. [2014] has been the first to characterize in general terms this query paradigm, and proposed then a practical solution for the case in which the user example is a substructure (a subgraph) of the knowledge graph while providing as answers all other isomorphic subgraphs. Later, this approach has been extended in Mottin et al. [2016] in order to allow for a different congruence relation, namely, strong simulation [Ma et al., 2014]. Formally, the exemplar query search problem is defined as follows.

Definition 3.10   Exemplar Query [Mottin et al., 2016].   The evaluation of an *exemplar query* represented by the sample s on a graph G, denoted as $xmpEval(s)$, is the set $\{a \mid s \approx a\}$; where a and s are elements in G, and the symbol $\approx$ indicates a congruence relation between elements, i.e., it states whether two elements are similar or not.

The exemplar query paradigm is the only one, up to this point, which accepts and exploits actual graphs as input examples. To implement such paradigm, we require first an appropriate *congruence relation*, i.e., the relation that is used to identify what subgraphs match the user intention, and then a fast retrieval system that can identify and return answer graphs.

As mentioned earlier, the works by Mottin et al. [2014] and Mottin et al. [2016] identify two viable congruence relations: edge-label preserving graph isomorphism and edge-label preserving strong simulation.[4]

Definition 3.11 A graph G is edge-label preserving *isomorphic* to a graph G', denoted as $G \simeq G'$, if there is a bijective function μ from the nodes of G to the nodes of G' such that for every edge $n_1 \xrightarrow{\ell} n_2$ in G, the edge $\mu(n_1) \xrightarrow{\ell} \mu(n_2)$ is in G'.

Edge-preserving isomorphism is a very restrictive congruence relation, in that it recognizes only exact structures. A more permissive type of graph homomorphism is *simulation* [Park, 1981]. However, *simulation* offers too few guarantees on the structure of the matched graph, and for this reason, strong simulation is preferred [Ma et al., 2014].[5] In Figure 3.10 we see an example of such properties. Assume $G1$ is a query, by adopting simulation, all $G2, G3, G4$ are matched. However, in $G3$ the fundamental property that the acquired and the acquiring company have both the same type (here *IT Companies*) is lost, since simulation does not require to match nodes with the same parent. In $G4$, simulation also matches disconnected graphs. With strong simulation only $G2$ matches all these characteristics, while still being flexible in some of the matched properties. Note that Strong simulation is not a symmetric relation.

The exemplar query approach for knowledge graph search is specially designed for very large datasets. The first part of the approach is an exact pruning technique, similar to many filtering approaches for graph search, called *neighborhood-based pruning*. The core idea is to represent each node, both in the query and in the graph, with a vector of numbers that summarize the edges around it. Consider $N_m(n)$ to be the set of nodes reachable with path of length exactly m from n. Given a predefined maximum distance d, for a node n, for every label ℓ and for every distance $i \in [1, ..., d]$ we keep the cardinality of the set $W_{n,\ell,i}$, where

$$W_{n,\ell,i} = \{n_1 | n_1 \xrightarrow{\ell} n_2 \vee n_1 \xleftarrow{\ell} n_2, n_2 \in N_{i-1}(n)\}.$$

As a result, a node vector $\mathbf{v}_n$ for the node n is a $1 \times (|\mathcal{L}| \cdot d)$ vector, with each position $\mathbf{v}_n^{\ell,i} = |W_{n,\ell,i}|$ containing the number of nodes reachable with an edge labeled ℓ as last step of a path of length i. Fast comparison among node vectors allows for effective pruning of candidate nodes. That is, we check if a node $n \in V_G$ can be a match for a node $\bar{n} \in V_Q$ by comparing $\mathbf{v}_n$ and $\mathbf{v}_{\bar{n}}$. In particular, it must hold that

$$\forall i \in [1, ..., d] \forall \ell \in \mathcal{L}. |W_{\bar{n},\ell,i}| \leq |W_{n,\ell,i}|.$$

In practice, a preprocessing step performs a BFS visit to each node in the graph and counts at each level the number of edge labels with a specific label. Then, those are stored in

---

[4]A more comprehensive survey of possible congruence relations for graphs is presented by Gallagher [2006] and Mennicke et al. [2017].

[5]See Ma et al. [2014] and footnote 4 for an analysis of the advantages and disadvantages of different congruence relations.

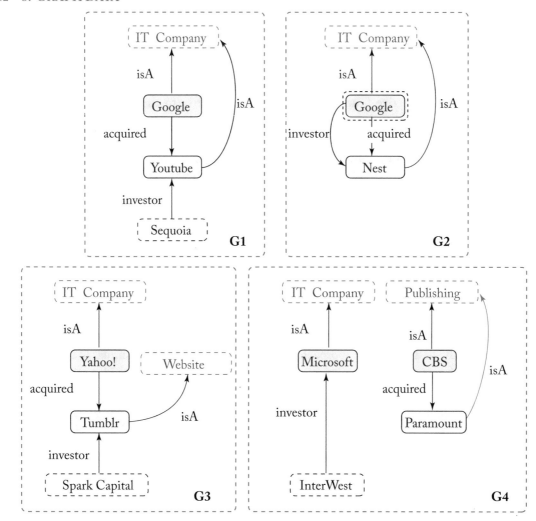

Figure 3.10: Example of simulating (G1~ {G2,G3,G4}) and strong simulating graphs (G1≈G2).

concise integer vectors, following a predefined order. Those vectors are quickly computed on-line for the query instead. By comparing a vector for a query node, with the vector for the nodes in the graph, it is possible to immediately discard any node that cannot possibly take part in any solution. This approach works both for isomorphism and for strong simulation, with only minimum modifications in how the comparison is performed.

Even when applying this type of pruning, the number of answers retrieved is usually considerable, and for this reason hardly processable by the user. For this reason, they propose an effective scoring and ranking technique that also offers significant pruning power. In particular, according to what we have already seen at the beginning of this chapter and in other works, it is assumed that the structures that are located in the graph in the proximity of the user example, are also the most relevant for the user. The approach followed in Mottin et al. [2014, 2016] scores the nodes around the query with a Personalized Page Rank [Jeh and Widom, 2003] computation, then based on some user-defined scoring threshold it prunes the portion of the graph that has a score below the threshold. Hence, only those nodes with a score above the threshold are taken into account as relevant for the user.

Multi-Example Search. Finally, a recent extension of the exemplar query paradigm by Lissandrini et al. [2018b] proposed, for the first time in the context of graph search, the problem of search via multiple examples. In this case, in contrast with all other methods presented up to this point, each one of the examples provided by the user is assumed to present one aspect of the desired result-set (see Figure 3.11). Hence, each example per se may be incomplete and as such it will not be part of the final answer-set. Yet, each element in the result should present all the characteristics of each example, combined in some way. The problem, similar to the original exemplar query work for the single example, is then formalized as follows.

Definition 3.12   Multi-Exemplar Query: mExQ.   The result of a *Multi-Exemplar query* for the set of samples S on a graph G, i.e., $mExQ(S)$, is the set $\{a \mid \forall s \in S.a \approx s\}$, where a and s are elements in G, $\forall s \in S.s$ is a subgraph of G, and the symbol $\approx$ indicates a congruence relation.

The naïve solution requires a subgraph-isomorphism search for each sample $s \in S$, in this way $n = |S|$ sets of subgraphs will be retrieved. Then, the final answer-set is a subset of the cartesian product of all the sets $A_1 \times A_2 \times \ldots A_n$, where A_i is the set of graphs isomorphic to the sample $s_i \in S$.

The naïve approach is far from scalable in general. Hence, they propose some optimizations that are still able to retrieve the complete set of answers. As it happens in the search for a single example, also in this case, the set of answers is too large to be of any use for the user. To tackle this issue, Lissandrini et al. [2018b] propose a flexible technique for finding only the top-k answers, given a generic relevance function. They assume a scoring function assigning scores to each node in the graph. These scores may represent proximity in the case of a PageRank or personalized page rank score. Alternatively, they may represent the result of some relevance function based on any external information, like user preferences, or popularity.

Equipped with these scores, they first select one sample among those provided in the query, then they retrieve a set of candidate nodes matching the chosen sample. These candidate nodes are treated as seeds. Exploration and search is then performed around each seed, one by one. At every moment an upper-bound score is kept for the maximal score obtainable by answers found around each seed. Such upper-bound allows for early termination of the search process when k answers have been found, and when no answer with a higher score exists.

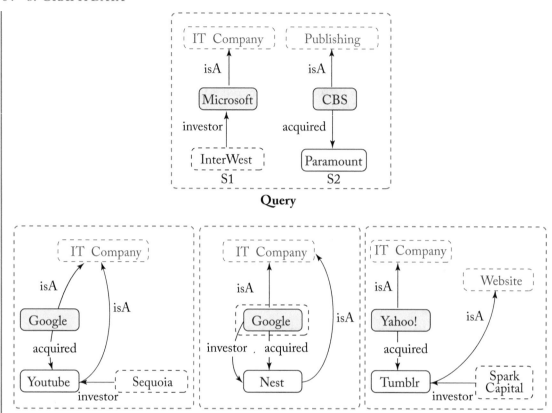

Figure 3.11: Example of multi-exemplar query (top) and answers (bottom).

Challenges and Future Directions: Graphs represent *connected elements*, and the ability to represent connections of different types (and how they combine in complex structures) is undoubtedly the feature that enabled the success of this data model. Therefore, to explore a graph is to explore the connections and structures it contains. As it is cumbersome for a user to specify those as examples, one could combine the translation of examples into structures (we have seen the work by Arenas et al. [2016] and Bonifati et al. [2015], and also the work by Jayaram et al. [2015]) with the composition of simple structures into more complex ones (as proposed by Lissandrini et al. [2018b] and Xie et al. [2017]). **The missing link, then, is an end-to-end approach, that can start from single nodes** (easily obtainable with traditional keyword-query mechanism), **construct partial structures** (e.g., with support of approximate graph matching techniques like the one by Khan et al. [2013]), and **allow for interactive and approximate explorations**.

Moreover, exploratory search needs may benefit from profiling, summarization, and aggregation techniques. Solutions like those proposed by Čebirić et al. [2015] and Song et al. [2016], should be integrated into a graph exploration system, **to provide, for instance, a concise and more approachable representation of the results of an exploratory query**.

3.5   SUMMARY

In this chapter, we surveyed methods that accept examples to enable exploratory search over large graphs. These by-example methods are particularly useful in the context of graph search, not only because they allow bypassing the need to adopt complex graph query languages, but also because they enable to exploit both explicit information stored in the graph and characteristics that can be inferred by the topology of the network.

We present a summary of such methods in Figure 3.12, where we divide the methods into two main groups, depending on what the target of the search is: (i) methods that we can adopt when the object of the search is a set of nodes and (ii) methods that are used to identify structures of interest.

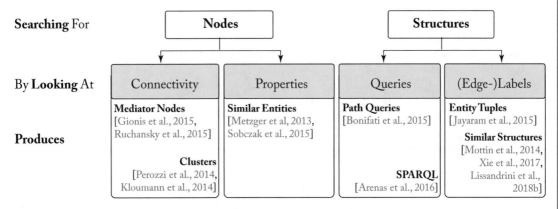

Figure 3.12: The different types of search techniques on graphs.

In the exemplar query paradigm, the input is examples of the result-set, and to retrieve the rest of the answers we need to specify a "*similarity function*" or a "*congruence relation*" that allows us to distinguish between relevant and irrelevant answers. In graphs, the similarity between the user example and the members of the result-set (in the case of nodes) may be just some form of proximity, as in the works of Gionis et al. [2015], Perozzi et al. [2014], Ruchansky et al. [2015], and Kloumann and Kleinberg [2014]. In this case, given a set of nodes, the topology of the graph is the only kind of information that we can explore, and the results will provide us with nodes that either have some critical role within the network or are members of the same community or cluster.

When the graph model is richer, i.e., when it contains properties, then the works of Metzger et al. [2013] and Sobczak et al. [2015] can exploit similarity between the features of the nodes in the user input and the desired answers. In this case, the methods allow us to identify entities that are similar because they represent entities with similar characteristics.

When dealing with structures, we can exploit methods that can identify more complex relationships between the user examples and the desired result-set. In particular, one the one hand, methods like those studied by Bonifati et al. [2016] and Arenas et al. [2016] can reverse engineer path queries and SPARQL queries from partial query specifications. Hence, by accepting as input nodes and node properties, respectively, they can identify a graph query that can return both nodes and structures with similar characteristics. On the other hand, the approach with entity tuples of Jayaram et al. [2014], and single and multiple exemplar queries, as proposed by Mottin et al. [2016] and Lissandrini et al. [2018b], identifies sets of relevant subgraphs without the need for graph query formulation.

CHAPTER 4

Textual Data

In this section we move our attention to repositories of unstructured data, i.e., *documents*. This includes repositories of scientific papers, documents crawled from the Web, forum posts, social media postings, and other similar collections of *textual-data*.

When searching those repositories we may want to find information at different levels of granularity. That is, we may be interested in finding documents that are similar to other documents we know to be relevant to our needs [El-Arini and Guestrin, 2011, Jia and Saule, 2017, Liu et al., 2003, Papadimitriou et al., 2017, Zhang and Lee, 2009, Zhu and Wu, 2014, Zhu et al., 2013], we may look for sentences or fragments of sentences describing specific types of concepts of which we know some instances [Agichtein and Gravano, 2000, Hanafi et al., 2017a,b, Ritter et al., 2015], alternatively, in more special cases, we may be willing to identify semi-structured information stored in the form of tables embedded within web-documents, i.e., web-tables [Wang et al., 2015, Yakout et al., 2012]. Hence, the techniques and applications covered in this chapter tackle the critical challenge of identifying portions of textual data that provide information similar to that described by some (possibly annotated) set of documents (or fragments of documents) given as examples.

Example 4.1 Brand X is considering to start producing a new product. Jodi then would like to gather reviews and customer opinions for similar products to understand their possible competitors. The typical approach to obtain such information would be to search on the Web for descriptions and reviews of similar products. However, it is tough to identify such pages since the search engine is returning thousands of results, and some competitor products may be missed if they are described differently. What if Jodi could merely identify some relevant web pages, and then ask the search engine to produce a more focused list of results (Section 4.1)? Alternatively, Jodi could fill up a small list of brands and name of products, and let the system crawl the web pages containing more elements of the same type (Section 4.2).

Textual information is one of the most abundant resources on the Web (let's think of web pages and posts on social media), one of the most easy to produce (since it doesn't require any technical competence), but given its unstructured nature, text is also very challenging to be mined and understood. An important observation is that documents may carry additional information that goes beyond the text they contain and which is usually present in form metadata. For instance, in the case of repositories of scientific papers, co-citation and co-authorship annotations provide insights into how those documents are connected. Web documents provide information in the form of hypertext links, sometimes the language itself features some regularities (patterns) that can be exploited for recognizing particular pieces of information, and (as mentioned earlier) in some case they contain semi-structured data in the form of tables. Hence, different aspects can be exploited to identify when two documents (or two fragments) may satisfy a similar information need.

Throughout this chapter, we will investigate how we can exploit both plain text data and meta-data, to identify the desired result set. We will show solutions for retrieving either full documents (Section 4.1) or semi-structured information (Section 4.2).

Exploring Documents: Repositories of unstructured or semi-structured text are ubiquitous. Web pages on the World Wide Web, or just within an institution domain, papers in an online repository or the archives of a journal, technical reports, documentation, posts in forums, online communities, and question-answering platforms.

These are rich, large, and extremely hard to query because the information they contain is unstructured. Most of the times a user only knows some keywords that describe some of the relevant documents, but many more documents do not contain those keywords. In other cases, the user is unsure about which keywords to use, but aware of a specific set of documents to be relevant for their search. In other cases, the user may know some specific instances of the type of information they are looking for, e.g., name and address pairs.

Exploring textual data by providing sample documents or sample text is then a natural approach, although the ambiguity of text and the lack of structure in the dataset needs to be compensated by other means.

4.1   DOCUMENTS AS EXAMPLES

Within a repository of documents, the most common task is to retrieve a set of documents that are relevant to a specific information need. In these cases, traditional search engines allow the user to express such need using a small set of keywords. It is often hard to describe a confused information need with just a few words, and often the result suffers either for a poor recall (for overly specific queries) or for poor precision (when the chosen keywords are very frequent in the repository).

Document search *by example* allows users to specify their information need as a set of exemplar documents rather than as a set of keywords. This method is useful for the cases in which the user is aware of a limited set of documents that are relevant to their search. These may be the subset of the result of an initial keyword-query search, and the desired result-set contains more documents of the same kind. Hence, the crucial task is how to discriminate when two documents contain related information.

Problem 4.2 Example-based Document Search Given a corpus of documents $\mathcal{D}$, and a small set of relevant documents ($\mathbf{D}_{rel}$), the problem of *Example-based Document Search* requires identifying a set of answer documents $\mathbf{D}_A$ such that $\mathbf{D}_{rel} \subseteq \mathbf{D}_A \subseteq \mathcal{D}$.

In these methods, document similarity may be guided by comparing the words each item contains (Section 4.1.1); alternatively, additional information may be exploited in order to represent pairwise relationships among documents and create in this way a network of documents (Section 4.1.2) that can be appropriately traversed.

4.1.1 LEARNING RELEVANCE FROM PLAIN-TEXT

In the context of document search, in general terms, the problem of retrieving a set of documents given an initial set of relevant (exemplar) documents has been approached in many different ways. In particular, many works have modeled the problem as a classification task, where the goal was to train a classifier able to assign each document either to the *relevant* class or to the *irrelevant* class. In this formulation, the primary challenge is that the user gives no member of the *irrelevant* class. Other approaches have extended this technique by extracting from the corpus a set of topic-labels, in this way the documents are enriched with information about the topics they match, and this information can be exploited by the classifier or by a pre-filtering step. Finally, a more advanced approach allows to decompose a single text in segments, and analyze the content of every single segment. Through this, the similarity across the documents is calculated through the similarity across the respective segments.

Text Classifiers Using Positive and Unlabeled Examples

Given a set of documents known to be relevant and the goal to identify other relevant documents from a corpus, the document classification task is formalized as follows [Liu et al., 2003].

Problem 4.3 Positive Unlabeled learning (PU learning) Given a corpus of documents $\mathcal{D}$, that can be classified as either relevant $\top$ or irrelevant $\bot$, a small set of few relevant documents ($\mathbf{D}_{rel}$) provided by the user (i.e., $\forall d \in \mathbf{D}_{rel}.class(d) = \top$), and considering the remaining documents as unlabeled data (i.e., $\mathbf{U} = \mathcal{D} - \mathbf{D}_{rel}$), the problem of *Positive Unlabeled learning* requires to train a classifier $\mathbb{C} : \mathcal{D} \mapsto \{\top, \bot\}$, such that it predicts the class $class(u)$ for each unlabeled document $u \in \mathbf{U}$.

To solve such problem the common approach can be summarized into two steps (Algorithm 4.9): first automatically select a subset $\mathbf{D}_{neg} \subseteq \mathbf{U}$ of (reliably) negative documents, i.e., a small set of documents to which we can assign the *irrelevant* label with sufficient confidence, then train the classifier $\mathbb{C}$ exploiting both $\mathbf{D}_{rel}$ and $\mathbf{D}_{neg}$. The training step is usually carried out as an iterative process, during which different versions of $\mathbb{C}$ are trained and also $\mathbf{D}_{neg}$ is updated accordingly.

Algorithm 4.9 Document Classification with Positive and Unalabled Data

---

Input: Relevant Documents $\mathbf{D}_{rel} \subseteq \mathcal{D}$, Unlabeled Documents $\mathbf{U} \subseteq \mathcal{D}$
Output: Classifier $\mathbb{C}$
1: $\mathbf{D}_{neg} \leftarrow$ getNegativeSample($\mathbf{U}$)   ▷ See Li and Liu [2003], Liu et al. [2002], Yu et al. [2002]
2: $\mathbb{C} \leftarrow$ trainClassifier($\mathbf{D}_{rel}, \mathbf{D}_{neg}, \mathbf{U} \setminus \mathbf{D}_{neg}$)   ▷ E.g., Expectation Maximization, SVM, or Rocchio
3: **return** $\mathbb{C}$

Adhering to this two-step process, Liu et al. [2003] study different combinations of methods to implement each step. For the first step, the methods investigated are Naïve Bayes [Mc-Callum et al., 1998], the Rocchio technique [Raskutti et al., 2002], the Spy technique [Liu et al., 2002], and th 1-DNF technique [Yu et al., 2002]. In *the Naïve Bayes* approach the entire set of unlabeled data ($\mathbf{U}$) is assumed to be negative, then a Naïve Bayes classifier is learned on top of this dataset exploiting the words in the documents as features, so that the probability $P(c_j|d_i)$, for $c_j \in \{\top, \bot\}$ and $d_i \in \mathbf{U}$ is estimated by means of the probability of $P(w_t|c_j)$, for $w_t \in \mathcal{W}$, where $\mathcal{W}$ is the dictionary of all the words appearing in the corpus $\mathcal{D}$.

The *Rocchio technique* instead represents documents as *tf-idf* vectors, and constructs a prototype vector $\vec{c}_j$ for each class. *Tf-idf* stands for *term frequency—inverse document frequency* (see Leskovec et al. [2014]). In this model, given a dictionary of words $\mathcal{W}$ of size $m = |\mathcal{W}|$, each document d of a corpus $\mathcal{D}$ is represented as a vector $\vec{v}$ of size m, where each position v_i stores a value proportional to the ratio between the frequency within d of the word $w_i \in \mathcal{W}$, and the number of documents that contain w_i in the entire corpus $\mathcal{D}$. Hence, the vector for the positive class $\top$ is $\vec{c}_\top$ and is computed with the formula

$$\vec{c}_\top = \alpha \frac{1}{|\mathbf{D}_{rel}|} \sum_{d \in \mathbf{D}_{rel}} \frac{\vec{d}}{||\vec{d}||} - \beta \frac{1}{|\mathbf{U}|} \sum_{d \in \mathbf{U}} \frac{\vec{d}}{||\vec{d}||},$$

where α, β are parameters to adjust the relative impact of the two sets [Raskutti et al., 2002]. The prototype vector for $\vec{c}_\bot$ is computed analogously to $\vec{c}_\top$. With this method, the vector representation of each document is compared via cosine similarity to the vector representation of each class, and the class is assigned to each document according to the highest similarity.

The *Spy technique*, instead, removes a small sample $\mathbf{S}$ of documents from those known to be relevant, i.e., $\mathbf{S} \subset \mathbf{D}_{rel}$, and includes them into $\mathbf{U}$, then trains a classifier as explained above for the Naïve Bayes method by treating $\mathbf{S} \cup \mathbf{U}$ as the set of negative examples. Once the classifier is trained, it exploits the documents in $\mathbf{S}$ to identify a probability threshold above which it can confidently assign the irrelevant label to the documents in $\mathbf{D}_{neg}$ [Liu et al., 2002]. Finally, *the 1-DNF* method, proposed by Yu et al. [2002], identifies as a set of words that appears more frequently in the labeled set $\mathbf{D}_{rel}$ than in the rest of the documents. These words are called positive features, and the set $\mathbf{D}_{neg}$ is composed of all those documents that do not contain any of those. All the methods above, then, devise some straightforward classifier to retrieve the small set of documents $\mathbf{D}_{neg}$ that are likely to be irrelevant.

The second step, instead, builds on the result of the first step to train a much more sophisticated and precise classifier. In this case, the methods investigated by Liu et al. [2003] comprise both expectation maximization (EM; Dempster et al. [1977]) and Support Vector Machines (SVM; Vapnik [2013]). In particular, they experiment with three different kinds of SVM, namely, a one-shot approach, where SVM is trained only once with $\mathbf{D}_{rel}$ and $\mathbf{D}_{neg}$, and two iterative methods where the SVM classifier is first trained and then used to extract a new set of documents to expand $\mathbf{D}_{neg}$. The new set is then exploited for another round of training until convergence (i.e., until no new document is added to $\mathbf{D}_{neg}$). Of the two variants of iterative training, the second one has a final step where the quality of the classifier at convergence is tested against the set $\mathbf{D}_{rel}$, and if the precision on $\mathbf{D}_{rel}$ is lower than 8% the classifier is discarded and the one trained at the first iteration is kept instead.

The conclusions in Liu et al. [2003] are that the methods they study are generally performing very poorly when the initial set of documents is very small (i.e., less than 10% of the entire set of relevant documents). In these cases the best method is the Rocchio approach for the first selection of the reliable negative samples, and expectations maximization for the training of the final classifier. SVM instead works best when the input set is much larger. More complex formulations of the Rocchio technique and SVM that are proposed in Liu et al. [2003] have also been studied by Zhang and Lee [2009]. In their work, they model each document with a *tf-idf* vector and train the SVM classifier only with positive examples by treating all the unlabeled examples as negative. Yet, the result does not differ much from the one by Liu et al. [2003].

While the major issue tackled by the approaches seen above is the absence of the negative set $\mathbf{D}_{neg}$, the work of Zhu et al. [2013] and Zhu and Wu [2014] focuses on the problem of the class unbalance between the cardinality of $\mathbf{D}_{rel}$ and $\mathbf{U}$. In particular, in Zhu et al. [2013] a set of m parallel under-sampling iterations are proposed, as a result m classifiers are learned, and the relevance of a document in $\mathbf{U}$ is then judged by aggregating all m distinct judgments. In Zhu and Wu [2014], instead, topic models (e.g., Blei et al. [2003]) are adopted to identify a subset of keywords that match the topics of the documents in $\mathbf{D}_{rel}$, these keywords are adopted to retrieve a subset of documents $\bar{\mathbf{U}} \subseteq \mathbf{U}$. In this way, only the documents in $\bar{\mathbf{U}}$ will be processed with the same PU techniques seen earlier. In general, from this set of studies, it appears that class imbalance is a huge source of noise which causes significant problems during the training of the classifier, while techniques that allow reducing the size of $\mathbf{U}$ allow for improvements in precision even for cases of small $\mathbf{D}_{rel}$.

Content Similarity based on Document Segmentation

The methods seen above exploited the frequency of words appearing in each document to identify the user need. Naturally, such an approach discards a significant amount of information that can be inferred by how words are combined and by the context in which they are used.

In particular, in Papadimitriou et al. [2017] documents are modeled as composite objects instead of monolithic entities. Different parts of the same document serve different intents and convey different messages. These parts are referred to as *segments*, and the task of identifying them alongside the goal they serve is called *Intention-Based Segmentation*. Indeed, Papadimitriou et al. [2017] tackle the problem of identifying a set of forum posts related to a specific post that the user knows to be relevant and provides as input. The context in which they study this problem is that of support forums. Those are communities where people can ask and obtain help from other users by discussing via forum posts. In these settings, users tend to ask for help by providing different kinds of information organized in the same text. For instance, in a post, one part of the text usually describes the problem that the author has, another provides some background information, and some other part may describe the desired outcome instead. By identifying these segments and classifying their goal, the meaning and importance of a term are estimated based on the segment in which the term is found.

Therefore, given an unstructured text, the primary challenge is how to identify the distinct segments. To this end, Papadimitriou et al. [2017] selects a set of text features whose presence or absence can correlate with different goals and *communication means*. The selected features are style, tone, brevity, verb tense, and other grammatical characteristics. Given a set of text features (summarized in Table 4.1 for the case of forum posts), intention-based segmentation measures the variation in their presence to identify the boundaries of each segment. The core concept in this task is the *Communication Mean* (CM), which is modeled as a categorical variable and its domain (the values it can assume) are specific textual features. For instance, the Subject CM can take one of three values: first person (I,We), second person (You), or third person (She,He,It).

Table 4.1: Features (cells) and Communication Means (rows) used for segmentation [Papadimitriou et al., 2017]

CM	Features		
Tense	Present	Past	Future
Subject	I/We	You	It/They/She/He
Style	Interrogative	Negative	Affirmative
Status	Passive	Active	
Part of Speech	Verb	Noun	Adjective/Adverb

Intuitively, a segment has a coherent distribution of features in its various CMs, e.g., in a segment the user always uses the third person and the past tense. Hence, in the procedure to segment a document, Papadimitriou et al. [2017] employs a bottom-up approach. First, it considers each single text unit (i.e., each word) as a separate segment. Then it scans all the segments to find those that can be merged. Two segments are merged if their richness increases while still presenting a similar distribution of values among the difference CMs. To this end, in the work of Papadimitriou et al. [2017], to evaluate a segment s_i they propose a *diversity index* as follows:

$$div(CM_x, s_i) = \sum_{f_x \in CM_x} \frac{f_x(s_i)}{|CM_x(s_i)|} \cdot \log\left(\frac{f_x(s_i)}{|CM_x(s_i)|}\right),$$

where CM_x is one of the communication means in Table 4.1, $f_x \in CM_x$ is a feature of CM_x and $f_x(s_i)$ is the number of appearances of that feature in the segment, while $|CM_x| = \sum_{f_x \in CM_x} f_x(s_i)$. Then, given the diversity index of a segment, the coherence of that segment is evaluated as

$$coh(s_i) = \frac{1}{|CM|} \sum_{CM_x \in CM} 1.0 - div(CM_x, s_i),$$

with CM being the set of all communication means in Figure 4.1. Hence, two consecutive segments s_i and s_{i+1} will be merged in one single segment $s_{i,i+1}$

$$iff. \quad coh(s_{i,i+1}) > coh(s_i) \land coh(s_{i,i+1}) > coh(s_{i+1}).$$

An example of segmentation is presented in Figure 4.1, with the number in the box representing the character position of the segment boundaries, and two types of CM are highlighted, namely verb tense and subject.

> [0]**I** have an HP system with a RAID 0 controller and 4 disks in form of a JBOD.[75] **I** would like to install Hadoop with a replication 4 HDFS and only 320GB of disk space used from every disc.[182] Do **you know** whether[201] **it** would perform ok or whether the partial use of the disk[259] would degrade performance.[285] **Friends** have downloaded the Cloudera distribution but[338] **it** didn't work.[355] **It** stopped since[371] **the web site** was suggesting to have 1TB disks.[418] **I** am asking because [436] **I** do not want to install Linux and then realize that[488] **my hardware configuration** is not the right one.[535]

Figure 4.1: An example of segmentation based on tense (underlined) and subject (bold) (from Papadimitriou et al. [2017]).

Once all documents have been segmented, segments of the same type, across documents, are clustered together. Clusters are formed by measuring the relative similarity of the distribution of features in the various segments. To this end, a characteristic vector is assigned to each segment, representing the presence and weight of each feature value for each CM. Then, traditional clustering techniques can be applied to identify clusters of segments with the same intention, i.e., with similar characteristic vectors. In the work of Papadimitriou et al. [2017], the clustering technique selected is DBSCAN [Ester et al., 1996] as it does not require to know the number of expected clusters and provides good resilience toward noise in the data. Then, given a document d_q, to retrieve a set of related documents D_{rel}, the system will segment d_q, identify for each segment the segments in the same cluster belonging to other documents, and the aggregate the similarity of those segments into a score for each document.

4.1.2   MODELING NETWORKS OF DOCUMENT

While the previous methods exploited only the contents (the words) of the documents to identify their relatedness, one could exploit an even richer set of features that are represented by meta-data and other attributes associated with them. In particular, in the following, we will see how we can model the connections among documents as a network. In this network, two documents are connected if one has influenced another (and vice versa) if one is linked to the other, if they have the same author, or if they are associated with the same topic. Hence, given a set of input documents, they become nodes in this network, and the answer documents to be returned can be identified by measuring some connectivity property (e.g., Page Rank).

In the following, we will investigate two distinct use-cases, namely, citation recommendations for scientific papers and document recommendations for web pages.

Citation Networks

In the work of El-Arini and Guestrin [2011], we find again the situation in which a user is aware of a set of document $\mathbf{D}_{rel} \subseteq \mathcal{D}$ that are relevant for their information need, and wants to retrieve from the corpus $\mathcal{D}$ a new set of answer documents $\mathbf{D}_A \subseteq \mathcal{D}$ relevant to that same need. On the other hand, here we expect $\mathbf{D}_A$ to maximize an *influence* score to and from the papers in $\mathbf{D}_{rel}$. Hence, documents in $\mathbf{D}_A$ are relevant if they are highly influential or influenced by the papers in $\mathbf{D}_{rel}$.

In particular, El-Arini and Guestrin [2011] models how a document d_i influences (or is influenced by) a paper d_j with reference to a topic or concept c_k. Hence, first, they identify a set of concepts $\mathcal{C}$ by retrieving important keyword from the corpus of documents (e.g., setting a threshold on the *tf-idf* values of the words present in each document). Then, for each concept $c_k \in \mathcal{C}$ they materialize a graph $G_k : \langle V, E \rangle$, where each node in V represents a document, and edges represent either citation or common authorship. Then, edges between documents are weighted relative to the number of documents they reference with the same concept, the number of documents authored by the same authors, as well as the total number of documents mentioning that concept. More formally, if a document $\bar{d}$ references papers $\{r_1, ..., r_n\} \subseteq \mathcal{D}$ and the authors of $\bar{d} \subseteq \mathcal{D}$ also authored papers $\{a_1, ..., a_m\}$, then the edge weights in G_k are assigned as follows:

$$\omega(r_i, \bar{d}) = \frac{1}{Z} \cdot \frac{freq(c_k, r_i)}{|r_i|}$$

$$\omega(a_i, \bar{d}) = \frac{1}{Z} \cdot \frac{freq(c_k, a_i)}{m \cdot |a_i|}$$

$$Z = \sum_{i \in [1,n]} \frac{freq(c_k, r_i)}{|r_i|} + \sum_{i \in [1,m]} \frac{freq(c_k, a_i)}{|a_i|} + novel(c_k, \bar{d}),$$

where $freq(c_k, d)$ is the frequency of concept c_k in the document $d \in \mathcal{D}$, $|d|$ is the number of words in the document d, and $novel(c_k, d) = freq(c_k, d)/freq(c_k, \mathcal{D}_{year})$ is the proportion of the frequency of c_k in d and the total frequency of c_k appearing in the subset of documents $\mathcal{D}_{year} \subseteq \mathcal{D}$ published in the same year as d.

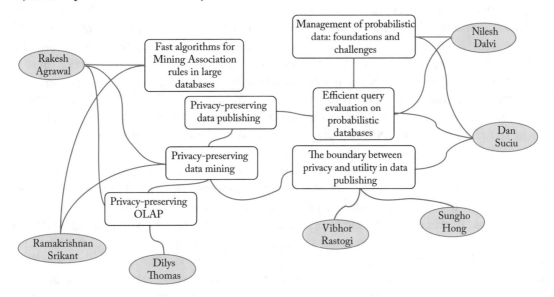

Figure 4.2: Example of citation Network.

Given the weighted graph G_k for concept c_k, El-Arini and Guestrin [2011] treats the weights on the edges of G_k as probabilities, so that, if there exist an edge $(d_i, d_j) \in E_k$, $\omega(d_i, d_j)$ is the likelihood of d_i having influenced d_j (and vice versa). Then, they formalize the *influence* between two documents d_i and d_j, as the probability that there exists a directed path in G_k between d_i and d_j. Since the problem to compute connectedness in a probabilistic graph is $\#P - Complete$, El-Arini and Guestrin [2011] identifies two strategies to compute such influence, namely via sampling and by applying a heuristic approach. In practice, the sampling approach materialized a version G'_k of G_k by randomly inserting or removing each edge $e \in E$ according to their probability $\omega(e)$. This process is repeated α times, and then the influence between d_i and d_j is proportional to the fraction of graphs G'_k in which a path exists between them. Interestingly, El-Arini and Guestrin [2011] proves that to estimate with sufficient confidence that the influence measure between any two documents is not too far away from its actual value, the number of sampling iterations should be proportional to $log(2 \times V)$. The heuristic approach, instead, assigns to each node a constant influence score and allows each node to transmit to the linked nodes a portion of that influence proportional to the edge weight connecting them. This approach reminisces Personalized Page Rank computation via particle filtering. Hence, the final influence between d_i and d_j is proportional to the influence score that started from d_i and reached d_j in this process.

Personalized Page Rank (PPR) is also one of the methods studied by Jia and Saule [2017]. In their study, Jia and Saule [2017] investigate the quality of the resultsets proposed for the paper recommendation task by different methods. Those methods are PaperRank (a version of Personalized Page Rank), CoCitation ranking, CoCoupling ranking, and Collaborative Filtering. As mentioned, PaperRank [Gori and Pucci, 2006] is a version of PPR where edges are weighted proportionally to the number of times a paper cites another paper. CoCitation and CoCoupling [Boyack and Klavans, 2010] are two complementary scores, the former scores the relevance of a paper $\bar{d}$ given a query-set of papers $\mathbf{D}_{rel}$ proportional to the number of times it was cited with the members of the query-set, while for the latter the score is proportional to the times it cites the same papers cited by papers in the query set. Finally, collaborative filtering [McNee et al., 2002] is a typical recommendation technique for recommending products to users. In the case of papers, the citing papers are treated as users, and the cited papers are treated as products.

Although all those techniques have been employed with some success for the paper recommendation task, Jia and Saule [2017] report that they offer poor precision and poor recall when it comes to long-tail papers, i.e., those papers that are not highly connected with many other papers. To this end, they study the *projection graph*, i.e., the subgraph induced by the citations of a paper. The projection graph shows how connected are the papers in the reference list of a given paper. By looking at it, they highlight how from an empirical study, about 50% of cited papers have only one, or no other links to the other co-cited papers, but the fact that they are cited together is a strong signal that they are reciprocally relevant. This calls for a more richer model, i.e., *just looking at citations and co-citations is not sufficient*.

In their work, they enrich the graph by also representing authors, keywords, and venues as nodes. Then, edges are added between papers and authors, authors and co-authors, keywords and papers, papers and venues in which they are published, and finally also authors and venues in which some of their papers have been published. Finally, given the set of query papers D_q, they run a Personalized Page Rank approach. This method proves to obtain a smaller recall, yet provides similar precision, but a much better diversity. That is, the top-k papers retrieved in this way are as relevant as those retrieved by more traditional approaches, but are also a completely distinct set, composed of papers that are more distantly connected by means of co-citation distance (i.e., they would be much harder to be retrieved by a user that was just looking at co-cited papers).

Related Web Pages

In search of documents on the Web, i.e., for all those cases in which we cannot exploit explicit meta-data like co-citations and co-authorship, we can still identify relatedness between documents by looking at the named entities appearing in them and also by exploiting click-logs and query-logs. Indeed, Bordino et al. [2013] presents a method to exploit this kind of information to suggest related searches based on the currently visited page.

In the use-case they envision, a user is currently visiting a specific web page (this page is then considered to be relevant to the current user need), then it is common that, after reading the page, the user may wish to expand their knowledge by searching for *related topics* which potentially come to mind *after* consulting the page. This navigate-and-expand process is a prototypical exploratory behavior (see White and Roth [2009]). Their goal is to suggest these *new queries* to the user, helping them in following their exploratory endeavor. Hence, those suggested queries should be *non-obvious* and *serendipitous*, that is, they should not describe the content of the current document (this will not provide new information), and should help the user find information about related topics that are not already covered by the current document.

To this end, the solution devised by Bordino et al. [2013] is to model a specific graph-model called *Entity-Query Graph* (EQGraph). The intuition behind it is the same that motivated the approaches mentioned earlier in exploiting the citation network and in enriching it with information about concepts. In practice, by following related concepts, the exploration can be guided by semantic-relatedness instead of being limited by syntactic similarities (i.e., considering only word co-occurrence or web links).

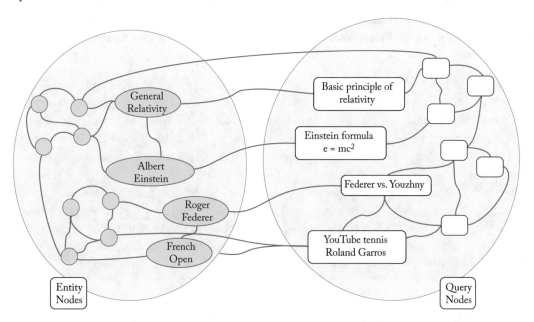

Figure 4.3: Example of EQGraph (based on Bordino et al. [2013]).

The EQGraph proposed in Bordino et al. [2013] is a graph $\langle N, E \rangle$, with two types of nodes: keyword-queries (N_Q) and named entities ($N_{\mathcal{E}}$), that is $N = N_Q \cup N_{\mathcal{E}}$ (see Figure 4.3). In this model, edges between queries are instantiated based on the query log, i.e., they insert an edge between the query node q_i and the query node q_j if the two queries are part of the same *search task*, that is when they are frequently used in the same search session. Then, edges between entities and queries are instantiated when a query q_i mentions an entity e_k. Finally, the EQGraph contains an edge between an entity e_k and another entity e_l, if there exists two queries q_k and q_l mentioning respective e_k and e_l and if there exist an edge (q_k, q_l) in the graph. Then, each edge in the EQGraph is weighted by counting the frequencies or the probabilities of such connections, e.g., $\omega(q_k, q_l)$ is relative to the portion of search sessions containing the two queries (q_k, q_l).

Given a page p and the EQGraph, the approach of Bordino et al. [2013] is defined in three steps.

1. Extract the *seed set of entities* $\mathcal{E}_{(p)} \subseteq N_\mathcal{E}$ from p.

2. Retrieve an *expanded* seed set $\mathcal{E}_{rel}$ such that $\mathcal{E}_{(p)} \subseteq \mathcal{E}_{rel} \subseteq N_\mathcal{E}$.

3. Obtain a set of queries $\mathcal{Q}_{rel} \subseteq N_\mathcal{Q}$ related to the expanded set of entities.

From the steps above, the first one can be solved with standard named entity recognition and disambiguation techniques (e.g., Wang and hua Fan [2009], Guo et al. [2009], and Ritter et al. [2011]), while the other two steps are solved (unsurprisingly at this point; see Chapter 3) via a Personalized Page Rank computation. The solution implemented by this process is then both proved to produce diverse and serendipitous suggestions and also to scale to large query logs and entity graphs.

Challenges and Future Directions: The exploration of a corpus of documents takes place at different levels. On one level, the search moves from one document to another. At the same time, each document provides information about one or more topics. Hence, the exploration moves from documents to topics, from a topic to related topics, and then back to documents. Topics and relatedness are broad terms that can be materialized in multiple ways. For instance, in this chapter, we have seen both word-similarity techniques and co-citation networks. Machine learning approaches constitute a new set of tools that can be adopted in this context (see Chapter 6) as well as the integration with rich knowledge graph (see Chapter 3). **Therefore, the study of document representation techniques that allow for richer semantic similarity, and the application of advanced models for text understanding, are required for improving the exploration of unstructured text.**

4.2   SEMI-STRUCTURED DATA AS EXAMPLE

In this second part of this chapter we will move to the challenging task of extracting (semi-)structured information from (almost-)unstructured text, and to use examples to guide this search. In particular, we will describe both approaches to identify pieces of text describing particular types of relations (Section 4.2.1), and also approaches that will try to navigate web-tables in order to retrieve both relations of the same type but also to retrieve the missing information needed to complete such relations (Section 4.2.2).

4.2.1   RELATION EXTRACTION

Relation Extraction refers to the task of distilling structured knowledge from unstructured text. The goal is to transpose knowledge from documents, which are hard to query, to tables (i.e., to a model compatible with the relational model see in Chapter 2) where a query system more easily accesses them. A relation extraction system is usually implemented by adopting a set of *extraction rules*, that is, a particular kind of regular expressions that identify the snippets of text describing the desired piece of information and how to extract its main components.

Example 4.4   Assume a set of news articles from a business-related website. To extract and fill a table listing organizations and the location of their headquarters, one could define the following set of extraction rules:

- "⟨E1⟩'s *headquarters in* ⟨E2⟩,"

- "⟨E1⟩, *based in* ⟨E2⟩," and

- "⟨E2⟩–*based* ⟨E1⟩."

Then, by parsing the set of articles and extracting the snippets of text matching the rules, the system could fill a table like Figure 4.4 by appropriately matching the respective placeholders ⟨E1⟩ and ⟨E2⟩.

Organization ⟨E1⟩	Headquarter ⟨E2⟩
Microsoft	Redmond
Google	Palo Alto
IBM	Armonk
Boeing	Seattle
Intel	Santa Clara

Figure 4.4: Organization/Headquarter relation.

A relation[1] is defined in the form of a set of tuples each with the form $t = (e_1, e_2, ..., e_n)$ where the elements $e_i \in t$ are entity mentions in a predefined relation *Rel* that appear within the document $d \in \mathcal{D}$. Most relation extraction systems focus on extracting binary relations as those in the example above, i.e., where each tuple has the form $t = (e_1, e_2)$.

Problem 4.5   Example-based Relation Extraction   Given a set of documents $\mathcal{D}$, a relation *Rel*, and a set of example tuples $T = \{t_1, t_2, ..., t_k\} \subseteq Rel$, the *Example-based Relation Extraction*

---

[1]Note that, here, the formal model of the output relation is similar to (and in a sense compatible with) the relational model, but it is not exactly the same.

problem requires to extract all other tuples $\bar{t} = (\bar{e}_1, \bar{e}_2,)$ such that there exists some sentence $S : \langle w_1, w_2, ..., \bar{e}_i, ..., w_j, ...\bar{e}_j, ..., w_n \rangle \in d \in \mathcal{D}$, with $e_i, e_j \in \bar{t} \in Rel$, and where $w_1, ..., w_n \in \mathcal{W}$ are words.

Relation extraction has been studied extensively since the early 2000s, and has proved extremely effective [Bach and Badaskar, 2007]. The hardest part of the task is to come up with an exhaustive and compelling list of extraction rules, and then to keep this list up-to-date. To overcome this problem, Agichtein and Gravano [2000] presents a semi-automatic relation extraction system called *Snowball*. Their approach, in turn, extends a previous system called DIPRE [Brin, 1998].

In the Snowball framework (Figure 4.5) the user can avoid specifying an initial set of extraction rules. Instead, the system can accept a set of *exemplar tuples*, that is a subset of the tuples to be found in the desired relation table (e.g., some rows of Figure 4.4 instead of the corresponding regular expressions). Given those tuples, the system will retrieve web pages that contain mention of those entities, extrapolate the snippets of text within which such mentions appear, and then construct the corresponding extraction rule. Then, such learned rules will be used to extract new tuples to fill the table (the relation), but hose new tuples will also be exploited as new examples that are fed to the system once more in an iterative process.

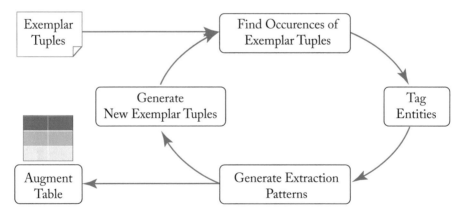

Figure 4.5: The Snowball Relation Extraction framework (based on Agichtein and Gravano [2000]).

A key advantage of the Snowball system is that the extraction rules they produce are actually *typed*. That is, for instance, in the pattern "⟨E1⟩'s *headquarters in* ⟨E2⟩", ⟨E1⟩ is actually annotated with the type Organization, while ⟨E2⟩ is annotated with the type Location. In this way, not any string will be matched by the rule, but only those that can match the appropriate type. Moreover, rules in Snowball are somehow flexible, i.e., specific tokens are assigned relative weights that allow partial matchings.

The critical element in the Snowball process, to ensure the quality of the information retrieved, is the dual process of generating new extraction rules and new tuples. It is essential to identify rules that allow good coverage of the instances contained in the corpus while avoiding introducing erroneous tuples in the output. Indeed, a set of erroneous tuples are likely to lead to invalid rules, initiating in this way a fatal vicious cycle. Therefore, in the work of Agichtein and Gravano [2000], they ensure the quality of an extraction rule r by first comparing the set of tuples extracted by it with the set of tuples already known to be correct. Intuitively, r should not generate any contradiction and possibly should extract some tuples that are already known. Similarly, also tuples can be validated, in particular, when the rule r extracts the tuple t, we should be able to identify a set of other rules $r_1, r_2, ..., r_k$ which also agree on extracting t from the corpus. These two intuitions define the confidence of a rule r and of a tuple t. Hence, by setting the minimum confidence threshold for a rule and a tuple, a user can define the *learning rate* of the system.

More recently, SEER [Hanafi et al., 2017a] extends the wealthy sets of systems and applications which build on the work of Snowball [Agichtein and Gravano, 2000] (such as Krishnamurthy et al. [2009], Li et al. [2015b]). SEER helps users extracting both extraction rules and relation tuples. In their work they propose to auto-generate information extraction rules via example tuples specified through a interface and an interactive system. The workflow of their approach is, in principle, analogous to the Snowball framework, while allowing user intervention. They extend the intuition behind the typed annotation in Agichtein and Gravano [2000]. They specify classes of rule tokens, namely: pre-builts, literals, dictionaries, gaps, and regular expressions. Those can match, respectively, specific types (e.g., names of organizations, people, phone numbers, addresses), exact strings (e.g., the literal string "percent"), list of specific literals (e.g., {"percent","%"}), characters to ignore (e.g., to skip between 0 and 3 characters), and actual regular expressions (e.g., "[A-Za-z]+"). An extraction rule is then defined as a sequence of rule tokens.

In SEER, the user is presented with some document that contains relevant information (e.g., retrieved via keyword search), and the user is asked to *highlight* in it the sentences that contain some of the relevant snippets. The sentence is then tokenized, and the different tokens are labeled with all the rule tokens that may apply (e.g., see Figure 4.6). All the possible interpretations are modeled within a tree in which a candidate rule is a path from the root to the leaf. Each rule token is assigned a priority or a preference so that a score can be computed for each rule. Then, only top-k rules will be presented as candidates to the user, and the user can select those that match their intent.

To help the user in their choice, the candidate rules are matched in the documents, so that a set of candidate matches are extracted and shown. In the SEER system, the user is also allowed to specify negative examples, those will also contribute to the refinement of the rules. The SEER system is hence expressive and advanced, allowing both for high coverage of the types of information extracted and also great usability since the entire process is both interactive and example-driven.

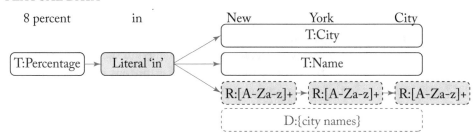

Figure 4.6: Possible tree generated for "8 percent in New York City" (based on Hanafi et al. [2017b].

Related Applications

Rule-based systems to extract ad-hoc information are extremely flexible and can be easily adapted to very specific use-cases. For instance, Ritter et al. [2015] proposes to adopt an example-driven rule-learning system to identify microblog posts that describe computer-security events. Their approach is weakly supervised, in the sense that they allow the user to specify a small number of seed examples, and from these, they learn rules to match other posts of the same type.

In their solution, an *event* is a tuple ⟨Topic, Entity, Date⟩, so that mentions of the event of type Topic are all those posts that match the keywords of the topic, mention the entity Entity, and are written in the specific Date. The topic is usually matched against a small set of topical keywords. In their approach, then, rules are composed by tokens that may describe the matched keyword, the named entity, literals, and Part-of-speech annotations (e.g., a matching rule may be of the form "PRP *hacked* Entity POS account"). In this way, each rule is encoded as a possible feature of the document, and then a PU approach (as those in Section 4.1.1) can be adopted to learn using them. In their system then, the example posts are adopted to learn topic-specific rules.

4.2.2   INCOMPLETE WEB TABLES

One of the *most structured* type of information contained in web-documents are *web-tables*. They are formatted within HTML specific markup, and this provides a good opportunity to extract information in the form of relations. *Entity-attribute tables* are a specific kind of web-tables containing values for multiple attributes of a set of entities, i.e., each row corresponds to an entity, and each column corresponds to an attribute for that entity (similarly to what presented in Figures 4.4 and 4.7).

The Web is full of this type of information, yet as it is already hard to identify relevant documents, identifying relevant web-tables can be even harder. Studies like Yakout et al. [2012] and Wang et al. [2015] present way to directly query a corpus of web-tables by allowing users to provide examples of the kind of information their are looking for.

T1

Name	Windows	Linux
Oracle	Yes	Yes
MySQL	Yes	Yes
SQL Server	Yes	No
PostgreSQL	Yes	Yes

OS support for top **database software**

T2

Name	License
MySQL	GPL
PostgreSQL	PostgreSQL
Firebird	IPL
Berkley DB	AGPLv3

List of Open Source **database software**

T3

Vendor	Revenue
Oracle	11787 M
IBM	4870 M
Microsoft	4098 M
Teradata	882 M

Database software, 2011 revenue by vendor

T4

Book	Price
SQL in 10 Minutes	20.03
SQL Server for Devs	38.13
Access 2013 Bible	32.15

Best-selling book on **database software**

T5

Name	Max Row Size
MySQL	64 Kb
Oracle	8 Kb
Firebird	64 Kb
Berkley DB	8 Kb

Information about **database** size limits

T6

Name	Developer
MySQL	Oracle
SQL Server	Microsoft
Office	Microsoft
Photoshop	Adobe

Best-selling **software** in 2010

Figure 4.7: Examples of web-tables for "database software," the text below the tables represent the caption found in the document.

Concept Expansion

In the work of Wang et al. [2015] they tackle a problem called Concept Expansion, which is analogous to the problem of Entity List expansion in knowledge graphs (see Section 3.2.3). The task they solve is formulated as follows.

Problem 4.6   Entity List Expansion [Wang et al., 2015]   Given a set of documents $\mathcal{D}$, a keyword-query Q describing an ad-hoc concept, and a small seed set of entities mentions $\mathcal{E}$ belonging to the concept, retrieve from $\mathcal{D}$ all the mentions $\mathcal{E}_Q$ for the entities belonging to the concept described by Q, such that $\mathcal{E} \subseteq \mathcal{E}_Q$.

To tackle the problem, Wang et al. [2015] exploits both the entity mentions and the keyword query to identify pages that contain web-tables that may be relevant for the user. Then, web-tables that contain the exemplar entity mentions are also likely to contain more mentions about relevant entities. There are cases in which entities are in the same table but for different reasons (i.e., see t6 in Figure 4.7). Hence, the challenge is recognizing which web-tables list entity mentions of the same type desired by the user. Since it is tough to discriminate precisely the relevance of a table, they adopt instead a probabilistic model where the top-k entities that are more likely to be relevant are returned.

The core model then connects entity-mentions with their appearances in a specific web-table. That is, they build a bipartite graph with entities and tables, where an edge $\langle e_i, t_j \rangle$ signals that an entity e_i appears within a specific table t_j. Notice that, in this model, the degree of an entity e_i provides information about how many tables mention that entity. Then, the information about the relevance of an entity is computed by navigating this graph and by exploiting the mentions of the entities provided by the user as positive examples. Moreover, additional information is exploited in this model, that is the relevance ranking (w.r.t. the user keyword query) of the page in which table t_j has been extracted.

Therefore, the approach of Wang et al. [2015] can be outlined as follows.

1. Build the bipartite graph.

2. Initialize the relevance of each table to a score $\sigma \in (0, 1]$ based on its ranking in the result-set of the user-specified keyword query.

3. Assign a score of 1 to each seed entity and initialize the output set **T**.

4. Propagate entity scores to each table in which they appear.

5. Select the table with the highest score and add it to **T**.

6. Propagate score from tables in **T** to the entities that appear in them.

7. Repeat from item 4.

In particular, Wang et al. [2015] provides an in-depth study of how to propagate the scores between tables and entities, and the heuristic adopted to avoid concept-drift, i.e., the mechanism by which, during an iterative process, a small error introduced during one step causes a substantial loss in precision in the following step. The main idea behind that approach is to favor tables that are very likely to contain only relevant entities, in contrast with what would have happened by applying a PPR approach.

Entity Augmentation

In Yakout et al. [2012], instead, web-tables are employed to retrieve essential attributes for a set of entities. That is, the input is a set of entity mentions paired with the name of the missing attribute, and the output is a table with the attribute value assigned to each entity.

Problem 4.7 Augmentation By Attribute Name   Given a set of web tables $\mathcal{T}$, a relation *Rel* defined by two attributes, i.e., $Rel = \langle a_1, a_2 \rangle$, and given some tuples $T = \{t_1, t_2, ..., t_k\}$, of which a subset is incomplete, i.e, $\bar{T} \subseteq T, t_i \in \bar{T}, t_i.a_2 = NULL$, the task of *Augmentation By Attribute Name* requires to retrieve all values for all the tuples in $\bar{T}$.

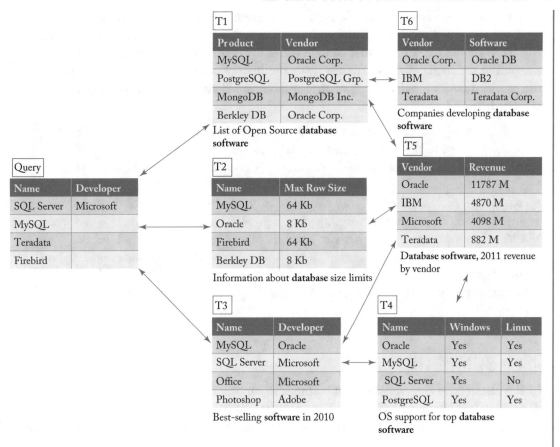

Figure 4.8: Example of web-tables graph.

For instance, the user may provide a set of company names (e.g., the companies in Figure 4.4), and the attribute name "Headquarter," and the system will fill that information for each of them. In the example in Figure 4.8, instead, the user query is a partially filled table about database software and vendors. Hence, while in the approach above each table were contributing only with the column in which the entity mentions of interest were appearing, here other columns from the web-tables are employed. In this case, then, the task will not require new entities of the same type, but new attributes to enrich the currently known entities. An interesting detail is that the approach [Yakout et al., 2012] can accept a set of example values for a subset of the entities in place of the attribute name.

To solve this task, the system devised in Yakout et al. [2012], called Infogather, build a graph where each node is a web-table, and edges connect similar tables with a score based on a schema-matching algorithm and on the similarity of the content of the web-pages in which they are embedded (see for example Figure 4.8). From this graph, candidate answer tables are retrieved via a PPR approach. The personalization vector needs to contain a set of seed tables, and those are the top-k tables that contain the entity mentions provided as examples. Then, by comparing the name of the attributes (with the help of a synonym-extraction technique), or the provided attribute values, a set of answer tables are identified and the corresponding values extracted.

Challenges and Future Directions: To distill structure from unstructured information allows for more effective management and querying of data. There is one constant in all the methods seen above: *entity mentions*. Relation extraction techniques and also the exploration of web-tables, are all developed around the concept of *entities*. For this reason, these methods are also crucial for knowledge graph construction (see for instance the work by Shin et al. [2015]). For the same reason, the use of knowledge graphs on one side and machine learning approaches on the other can be effectively exploited to tackle these tasks (see for instance the book by Nastase et al. [2013]). **The major challenge in this context is how to combine relation extraction techniques in an interactive work-flow that helps the user in finding answers to complex information needs that cannot be summarized by one simple n-ary relation.**

4.3   SUMMARY

In this chapter, we analyzed different methods to support exploratory search over unstructured documents (see Figure 4.9). One of the main challenges resides in the fact that text may be dense of information, but such information needs to be extracted in order to be processed by a search system.

As a matter of fact, when exploring document repositories, we may be either interested in retrieving some specific set of documents, in order to read or post-process them, or alternatively, we may wish to access directly some specific piece of information within them.

We reviewed techniques that can help in both the aforementioned cases. On one side, we may start our search from one or more documents that we know are relevant. In this case, we want to retrieve other documents that are similar, or related. To identify such documents, we may look at the textual content, the terms, and identify the topics that are of interest. These are the methods of Liu et al. [2002], Zhang and Lee [2009], Zhu et al. [2013], and Papadimitriou et al. [2017], which analyze words to automatically understand their intended topic, or the goal they express. Alternatively, related documents can be identified by looking at meta-data, e.g., links, citations, or at the entities they contain, and then by matching them with entities in other documents, or even query-logs. These are the solutions presented by El-Arini and Guestrin [2011], Jia and Saule [2017], and Bordino et al. [2013].

On the other side, we may be interested in semi-structured information that can be distilled from the contents of the corpus we are analyzing. Such semi-structured information may be presented in input as examples of entity mentions describing relations, or as (incomplete) web-tables. The approaches of Agichtein and Gravano [2000], Hanafi et al. [2017a], and Ritter et al. [2011] will identify the rules or patterns that are able to extract other entity mentions that satisfy the same relations. Instead, the solutions presented by Wang et al. [2015] and Yakout et al. [2012] allow to complete, enhance, or expand the provided tables.

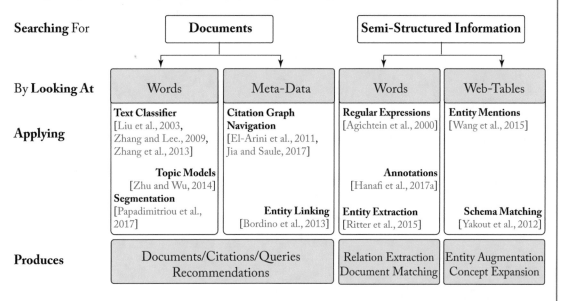

Figure 4.9: The different types of search techniques on textual data.

CHAPTER 5

Unifying Example-Based Approaches

The approaches presented so far are tailored to the three main data models, from fully structured data (relational), to semi-structured (graphs) and unstructured (textual) data. In the implementation of an exploratory system, the natural choice of the specific example-based technique to employ depends on the data model and the search task. However, in the case in which we need to query heterogeneous datasets, the choice of the right algorithm is harder. Appropriate cross-models techniques can sooth this issue. Unfortunately, only a few works favor a model-agnostic approach to the problem.

In this chapter, we reason about this issue and discuss possible unification approaches, through established research techniques. The information presented in this chapter offers a different perspective on the example-based approaches we addressed so far and should be considered as a preliminary step for unification, rather than a comprehensive framework. In Section 5.1, we unveil a body of research that translates information from one data model to another. In Section 5.2, we formally analyze the example-based approaches in the unifying view of the *relation seeking* task (as depicted in Figure 5.1), and reveal how a few key strategies are applied to solve it in different data-models. Finally, in Section 5.3, we highlight how the concept of *entity* (independently of the data model) and the family of methods employed for entity matching, resolution, and linking, are one more possible bridge that opens the way to multi-model exploration systems.

5.1 DATA MODEL CONVERSION

Data model translation deals with the problem of translating one data model into another. Such techniques try to preserve the information while converting its representation. However, there is some unavoidable loss of information in the translation phase, which in our case might hinder the application of the example-based techniques. While converting data from unstructured (text) to more structured (relational, graph) can lead to the discovery of new patterns, the reverse implies a loss of the schema and might result in poorly conceived descriptions.

In the following, we briefly describe a number of such techniques, summarized in Table 5.1.

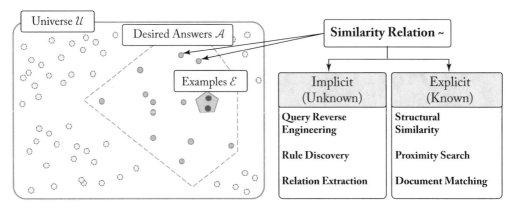

Figure 5.1: An overview of the example-based query paradigm and a summary of the search techniques over different data-models.

From relational.   Translating *relational data into graphs* is routinely done to enable processing techniques that can exploit this less structured data-model. The conversion is performed by considering foreign keys or join tables as edges among tuples. Therefore, many approaches can successfully represent relational databases as graphs. W3C guidelines provide a standard approach to represent relational data as RDF Knowledge graphs [Arenas et al., 2012]. In the same way, SQL queries are transformed to and executed on a graph [De Virgilio et al., 2013]. Besides explicit relationships, recent approaches [Xirogiannopoulos and Deshpande, 2017, Xirogiannopoulos et al., 2015] allow user-defined extraction of graph summaries from relational databases. In such summaries, exploratory analysis becomes more natural, since we deal with a more flexible schema that highlights connections among heterogeneous objects.

The conversion from *relational to text* results in a considerable loss of information, but enhances the readability of part of the data, which is essential for exploratory tasks. For instance, the Logos system [Kokkalis et al., 2012] produces easy to read explanations for SQL queries to novice users.

Still, obtaining a textual representation of a database facilitates common natural language search techniques to be applied for exploratory search over data from relational sources [Bergamaschi et al., 2011, Yu et al., 2010].

From graphs.   Graphs offer more flexibility than relational data at the price of a higher computational-cost for many data-analysis tasks and with the loss of some guarantees about the schema of the data. Hence, *relational representations of graphs* either tend first to discover functional dependencies on graphs [Fan et al., 2016], or directly store simple triples in one or

Table 5.1: Conversion of data from one model to another

From - To	Relational	Graph	Text
Relational	—	[Singh et al., 2015] [Orel et al., 2016] [Xirogiannopoulos et al., 2015] [De Virgilio et al., 2013] [Arenas et al., 2012]	[O'Donnell et al., 2000] [Kokkalis et al., 2012]
Graph	[Weiss et al., 2008] [Fan et al., 2016]	—	[Trisedya et al., 2018] [Gardent et al., 2017] [Perez-Beltrachini et al., 2016]
Text	[Zhang, 2008] [Agichtein and Gravano, 2000]	[Shen et al., 2015] [Lin et al., 2012] [Dong et al., 2014]	—

more tables [Weiss et al., 2008]. Discovering functional dependencies allows for a more expressive representation and reasoning than storing edges as triples.

On the other hand, *graphs (especially knowledge graphs) are translated to text* to support, for instance, smart assistants [Gardent et al., 2017, Perez-Beltrachini et al., 2016, Trisedya et al., 2018]. Such approaches use recent advances in neural methods to expand graph relationships and nodes to sentences and paragraphs.

From text.   The most popular transformation involves textual data represented into relational or graphs (as seen in Chapter 4). As we have seen, Snowball [Agichtein and Gravano, 2000] is one of the earliest approaches for entity and relation extractions from documents. Snowball belongs to the more general category of information extraction methods that lately included machine learning approaches [Zhang, 2008] as well, for the task of *relation extraction*. The methods are then widely used to extract machine-readable information and to expand data-repositories continuously.

Graph extraction from text aims at constructing knowledge graphs from document corpora. Notable examples of such methods include Knowledge Vault [Dong et al., 2014] and YAGO [Suchanek et al., 2007]. Similarly, entity linking induces graphs from documents by associating a node to each entity mentioned in a text [Lin et al., 2012, Perez-Beltrachini et al., 2016]. These techniques enable automatic and semi-automatic data extraction and exploration for user-generated content, like reviews, posts on social networks, and blogs [Song et al., 2011].

5.2   SEEKING RELATIONS

We now look to the general family of example-based approaches under the unifying perspective of inferring the relation that describes the user examples and, consequently, the desired answers. The central assumption behind example-based approaches is the existence of an answer set of desired items $\mathcal{A}$ from a universe $\mathcal{U}$. Naturally, such items comply with the data model and, as such, can take the form of tuples, pairs, members of a community, entities in a knowledge graph and so on. Nonetheless, independently from the data model, the user aims at identifying the members of $\mathcal{A}$ that has some characteristics, or distinguishing which properties characterize such set. As discussed earlier, the user may not be able to describe such characteristics. Yet, the user may know a small set of examples $\mathcal{E} \subseteq \mathcal{A}$ or, worse, a partial description $(\bar{\mathcal{E}})$ of those examples, where each $\bar{e} \in \bar{\mathcal{E}}$ share some characteristic with elements in $\mathcal{A}$, i.e., $(e \in \mathcal{A}, \bar{e} \approx e)$. A case of a partial description is, for instance, the case of tuples with some unknown values.

A natural assumption on the elements in $\mathcal{A}$ is to conclude a shared set of characteristics of interest among them. In other words, we assume that the elements in $\mathcal{A}$ are consistent with a tacit relation $\sim$ among each pair of elements $a_1, a_2 \in \mathcal{A}$. As such, independently of the data model, the methods in the previous chapters fall into two groups: first, when the similarity $\sim$ is *implicit* and unknown, and, second, when the relation $\sim$ is *explicit* and belongs to a parametric family of relations. As soon as the relation $\sim$ is either discovered or parametrized, the challenge in both cases is to retrieve all or the most relevant members of $\mathcal{A}$.

5.2.1   IMPLICIT RELATION

A relation is implicit when the desired elements (the answers) $\mathcal{A}$ belong to a query or an equivalence class, but such relation $\sim$ is not provided beforehand. Methods that assume implicit relations include query reverse engineering, presented in Sections 2.2 and 3.6, and the rule-discovery methods for schema mapping in Section 2.3, data cleaning in Section 2.4, and relation extraction in Section 4.2.1.

An implicit relation is represented by a set of queries that return answers $Q(\mathcal{U})$ containing the examples $\mathcal{E}$. The definition of an implicit relation is oblivious to the data model, as long as the results can be expressed as logic constructs. In general, for any data-model that can be queried through some formal query language, we can assume reverse-engineering progress that starts from the examples, generates possible query constructs that are satisfied by those examples, and then selects some or all of them to produce the final answer-set. Hence, matching rules fall in the same category, since they generalize the concept of queries.

Logic constructs apply to structured, or partially structured data, but fall short on textual data that expose no formal query language. For textual data, one should rely instead on information retrieval models [Roelleke, 2013].

Navigating Query Alternatives

Reverse engineering methods exploit the formalism of the query language and the properties of inductive reasoning starting from few query conditions to more refined queries, which include all the examples. Finding an adequately refined query is combinatorial in the number of query conditions. The more expressive the language and the data model are, the larger the number of queries that could satisfy the provided input is. In all these cases, even with rather simple query constructs, the computational complexity of just checking whether or not a query may satisfy the desired examples is often intractable. A set of assumptions are carried on the structure of the final queries to avoid such combinatorial explosion. Also, when the algorithm needs to materialize hundreds or thousands of queries, preference metrics, and greedy algorithms are employed to favor simpler queries or specific conditions on the result set. In all those cases, a common approach is to include positive and negative examples from the user. This problem formulation has proven to practically increase the control on the side of the user (even though it does not lead to more tractable problems).

5.2.2   EXPLICIT RELATION

Some methods explicitly require or define a relation or a similarity among items. Most graph and document search methods in Chapters 3 and 4 assume a relation among objects, such as structural similarity, proximity, or content similarity, whose nature is well defined and understood. On the one hand, these methods only require for some parameter to be derived from the examples, to tune such relation and instruct the search task. In these cases, the primary challenge is how to efficiently retrieve those elements belonging to the given (parametrized) relation. The community detection task [Gionis et al., 2015, 2017] and exemplar queries [Mottin et al., 2016], for instance, fall in this category. In other cases, even though the desired relation is known, to retrieve all answers that perfectly match it can be computationally expensive. In many other cases, the relation that describes the answers is not known and can only be guessed. In both of these cases, the task is then the discovery of a relation that approximates the desired one over the example items. Approaches like the one for focused clustering [Perozzi et al., 2014] and for document search Liu et al. [2002] fall in this category. A common approach to identify the link between the provided examples and the desired answers is precisely to identify similarity or relatedness relationships among the items in the dataset.

Similarity Networks

Applications in multiple domains have recognized how the search space can be modeled as a network of objects that can be connected by some similarity, or relatedness relation [Bordino et al., 2013, Hu et al., 2009, Shen et al., 2015]. Less structured data-models, such as documents and graphs, require approaches that discover when two objects are either similar (because they share attribute values or content), or exploit explicit information of when two items are related (e.g., via document links, or edges in a graph). Similarities provide convenient means to abstract data models and reason in the resulting similarity networks. Such *navigation* step, can exploit well known techniques like PageRank [Page et al.], Personalized Page Rank [Jeh and Widom, 2003], SimRank [Jeh and Widom, 2002], or measure actual proximity among nodes [Kloumann and Kleinberg, 2014].

Similarity networks can be used for all cases in which user requirements are ambiguous, or examples are underspecified so that the reasons for their relevance need to be inferred by external, or latent information. In some cases, these techniques are not apt to identify the desired result set, but only to prioritize or rank the answers in those cases in which only the most relevant should be returned.

Notably, while in some case explicit relationships already exist as links or edges, in some other cases they can be obtained by a preprocessing step through the analysis of meta-data, or by integrating external knowledge (e.g., taxonomies). More recently, representations of similarity networks in lower dimensional spaces, namely *graph embeddings* [Wang et al., 2017], have impulsed the study of similarities that are learned directly from the data. As a middle ground between explicit and implicit relations, similarity learning [Kulis et al., 2013] aims at specifically defining similarities from examples of similar and dissimilar item pairs. In this regard, Chapter 6 describes learning methods from unknown user preferences in an online manner.

5.3 ENTITY EXTRACTION AND MATCHING

In the approaches explored in the previous chapters, we have frequently encountered the concept of **entity** [Cheng, 2012, Lin et al., 2012, Shen et al., 2015], which refers to any object, person, concept, or event. An entity is uniquely identified, but the representation can vary across datamodels and formats. Identifying the entities mentioned by the user and their appearance in the dataset can significantly help the system understand the user intention [Guo et al., 2009, Song et al., 2011, Wang and hua Fan, 2009].

In particular, in exploratory methods for relational data, entity matching enables the retrieval of the correct instances that are desired as query results [Singh et al., 2017]. In such methods, *schema matching* techniques are a core step that can be employed precisely because of the presence of a schema.

For graph data, entities are usually the most common type of input; hence, to correctly answer the query, *entity matching* is the necessary step that is needed to understand the user's examples [Kargar and An, 2011, Khan et al., 2013]. Since entities relate to each other, similarities are first class citizens to retrieve the correct answers [Bordino et al., 2013].

Finally, within documents, multiple approaches exploited additional sources (e.g., knowledge graphs) to include entities mentioned in the text [Hu et al., 2009]. The preliminary step in such approaches is called *entity extraction*.

In summary, entities are a natural bridge between the user representation of the world and the semantic understanding of the system. As such, entity linking and entity resolution methods [Christophides et al., 2015, Papadakis and Palpanas, 2018] can be effectively exploited across multiple data models to enhance the capabilities of the system to understand the user intent and identify the desired answers. Such methods will be of vital importance in the task to allow cross-model explorations (see also Chapter 7) in all those repositories that store multiple data models (e.g., in the case of data lakes and polystores [Deng et al., 2017], and more complex hybrid analytical processes [Abelló et al., 2013]).

PART II

Open Research Directions

CHAPTER 6

Online Learning

Until now we have considered users as mere spectators of the algorithmic process, while their preferences influence the result of the algorithm. The algorithms in previous chapters assume fixed user preferences or refinement criteria based on hardwired rules. Even in those approaches that allow for an interactive work-flow, the system can infer only limited information about the user preferences, and still based on a fixed discovery approach. However, user preferences are undisclosed and different from user to user.

The current developments in machine learning and active search [Ma et al., 2015, Murai et al., 2017, Su et al., 2015] present a different perspective: user preferences can be learned from user interactions instead of manually crafted in the system, and the discovery process can adapt to the user. Current hardware capabilities allow to process a large amount of data, and at the same time dynamically change the internal preference model. One of the earliest work in this direction is MindReader [Ishikawa et al., 1998] in which the user specifies a set of tuples and optional relevance scores and the system infers a distance function on the objects in the database. The exploration of such *relevance learning* or *metric learning* approaches form the basis of interactive exploratory systems. Moreover, the study of Gaussian Processes as a mean of interactively learning any function given a set of points from the user has recently found applications in graphs [Ma et al., 2015, Murai et al., 2017].

Supervised machine learning relies on given labels to known data-items (e.g., stock values) to learn the parameters of a function (or model) that associates labels to unseen data points. Traditionally, supervised approaches have learned from already labeled data *offline* in a batch mode. We turn our attention to the more recent *online* methods, which progressively learn the parameters as new label comes. *Passive* online methods wait for the user to provide labels, while *active* methods select an unlabeled item from the dataset and ask the user evaluation. Figure 6.1 depicts the difference between offline and online learning.

We introduce now the notation used throughout the chapter that abstracts the three primary models studied in the previous chapters. A *dataset* is a set $\mathcal{X}$ of items $x \in \mathbb{R}^n$ in some n-dimensional. An oracle, such as a user, provides a label y_t at time t to one item $x \in \mathcal{X}$. The purpose is to learn the parameters of a family of functions (a model) $f^{\theta_t} : \mathcal{X} \to \mathcal{Y}$ parameterized by θ which assigns a label to each of the items in $\mathcal{X}$. The label set $\mathcal{Y}$ depends on the specific problem: for binary classification $\mathcal{Y} = \{-1, 1\}$, for regression $\mathcal{Y} = \mathbb{R}$ or $\mathcal{Y} = [0, 1]$, for multiclass classification $\mathcal{Y} \subseteq \mathbb{N}$, while for multi-label classification $\mathcal{Y} = \{0, 1\}^m$. This chapter, albeit not intended as an exhaustive dissertation of the subject, provides a useful overview of research

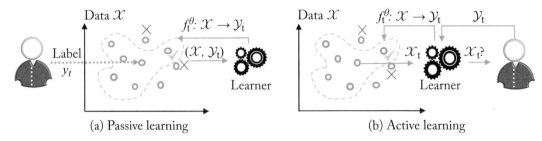

(a) Passive learning   (b) Active learning

Figure 6.1: Online learning strategies: active (a) and passive (b).

directions to improve the usability of example-based approaches. The research in this area is still in its infancy and forms a fertile ground for a new generation of data management systems. For an in-depth survey on online learning, we refer to Hoi et al. [2018].

This chapter offers an overview of online learning techniques that can be integrated into existing approaches to improve the results through explicit user-modeling. Section 6.1 introduces passive learning, where a learner waits for examples from a source, such as a user. Active learning, presented in Section 6.2, instead samples the examples from the database and ask the user to rate the results. We conclude with AIDE (Section 6.3), an example-based system based on learning, which can scale to large datasets.

6.1   PASSIVE LEARNING

Online passive learning is a sequential process in which on each round t a learner gets a new data instance x and makes a prediction $\tilde{y}_t = \text{sgn}(f_t^{\theta}(x))$, where sgn is the sign function, on such instance based on the current model. Passive learning is useful when data labels come in streaming fashion, and each iteration provides some more information about the model to learn because it avoids re-learning the model from scratch.

The model parameters θ are updated for each new data-point using a loss function L which quantifies the deviation of the predicted value $\tilde{y}_t$ with respect to the real value y_t. Algorithm 6.10 shows the procedure for learning a binary classifier in an online setting. The learning algorithms differ from one another from the choice of the model f, the loss function L, and the Update function.

In passive learning, users are deemed as information sources that provide at each iteration a label for an item of their choice. Hence, the system has no role in the selection of the data-item to label at each iteration. We present the different main methods for passive online learning, and then we overview MindReader, the first application to database systems.

Algorithm 6.10 Online binary classification

1: Initialize $\boldsymbol{\theta}$
2: **for** $t = 1, 2, ..., T$ **do**
3:     Get instance $\boldsymbol{x} \in \mathbb{R}^n$
4:     $\tilde{y}_t \leftarrow \text{sgn}(f_t^\theta(\boldsymbol{x}))$ ▷ Label prediction with current model
5:     Get correct label $y_t \in \{-1, 1\}$
6:     $\ell \leftarrow L(\tilde{y}_t, y_t)$ ▷ Loss on the prediction
7:     $\theta \leftarrow \text{Update}(\theta, \ell)$
8: **end for**

6.1.1   FIRST- AND SECOND-ORDER LEARNING

There are two main approaches to passive learning: first-order online learning and second-order learning. The main difference between first- and second-order online learning is the use of the gradients. In particular, second-order learning exploit the information in the second-order gradients to speed up the convergence.

The oldest first-order learning is the *perceptron* [Agmon, 1954]. The perceptron is a function $f(x) = \text{sgn}(\boldsymbol{\theta} \cdot \boldsymbol{x})$, which returns a binary value on a linear function $\boldsymbol{\theta} \cdot \boldsymbol{x}$. If the predicted value $\hat{y}_t$ is different from the actual value y_t for the data item $\boldsymbol{x}$ at time t, the parameters $\boldsymbol{\theta}$ are updated (Line 7, Algorithm 6.10) as follows:

$$\boldsymbol{\theta} \leftarrow \boldsymbol{\theta} + y_t \boldsymbol{x},$$

where such update follows the direction of the gradient of the loss for the prediction f.

A second-order improved version [Cesa-Bianchi et al., 2005] improves the convergence of the perceptron, by exploiting the covariance $\mathbf{M} = \sum_{t=1}^{T} \boldsymbol{x}_t \boldsymbol{x}_t^\top$ of the first T data items. The second-order is the original perceptron on the sequence $(\mathbf{M}^{-1/2}\boldsymbol{x}_1, y_1), ..., (\mathbf{M}^{-1/2}\boldsymbol{x}_T, y_T)$ which reduces the variance in the estimate. In fact, the correlation matrix is reduced to the identity $\mathbf{I}$

$$\sum_{t=1}^{T} \left(\mathbf{M}^{-1/2}\boldsymbol{x}_t\right)\left(\mathbf{M}^{-1/2}\boldsymbol{x}_t\right)^T = \sum_{t=1}^{T} \mathbf{M}^{-1/2}\boldsymbol{x}_t\boldsymbol{x}_t^T\mathbf{M}^{-1/2}$$
$$= \mathbf{M}^{-1/2}\mathbf{M}\mathbf{M}^{-1/2}$$
$$= \mathbf{I}.$$

6.1.2   REGULARIZATION

Online methods can become particularly slow when data are highly dimensional. To remedy such problem, some *regularization* on the parameters is introduced, which exploit the sparsity of high-dimensional data, a prerequisite for several optimizations. In general, regularization introduces additional penalties on the parameters to prevent overfitting. As such, regularization typically adds a factor that controls the sparsity of the parameter vector $\boldsymbol{\theta}$. This parameter minimizes the number of non-zero entries represented by the ℓ_0-norm $||\theta||_0$. Since minimizing the ℓ_0-norm is hard, the solution is to minimize instead the sum of absolute values of θ computed by the ℓ_1-norm $||\theta||_1 = \sum_{i=0}^{n} |\theta[i]|$.

Most of the methods propose fixed regularization terms that do not adapt to the underlying data distribution. The solution proposed by Duchi et al. [2011] profits from the second-order information accumulated during the process. The regularization to the second-order moments $H_t = (\sum_{i=1}^{t} \boldsymbol{g}_i \boldsymbol{g}_i^\top)^{\frac{1}{2}}$ is given by

$$h_t(\theta) = \frac{1}{2} \theta^\top H_t \theta,$$

where $\boldsymbol{g}_t = \frac{1}{t} \sum_{i=1}^{t} \nabla L_i(\theta^{(i)})$ is the average gradient of the loss function for the parameters $\theta^{(i)}$ at time $i = 1, 2, ..., t$.

6.1.3   MINDREADER

A notable database application of online learning theories is MindReader [Ishikawa et al., 1998]. MindReader introduced interactivity with the user to learn a distance function among items in a database and example items provided by the user, thereby inferring an implicit query expressed by weights over attributes. The learned distance function is a *generalized ellipsoid distance* which is more flexible than Euclidean.

MindReader assumes the user preferences are described by an undisclosed query point $\boldsymbol{q} \in \mathbb{R}^n$ represented as an n-dimensional vector. Given any other point $\boldsymbol{x} \in \mathcal{X}$, the quadratic generalized ellipsoid distance is

$$d(\boldsymbol{x}, \boldsymbol{q}) = (\boldsymbol{x} - \boldsymbol{q})^\top \mathbf{M}(\boldsymbol{x} - \boldsymbol{q}) = \sum_i^n \sum_j^n \mathbf{M}_{ij} (x_j - q_j)(x_j - q_j). \tag{6.1}$$

Such distance extends the Euclidean and weighted Euclidean, by introducing a weight matrix $\mathbf{M}$ along the different dimensions. Note that the Euclidean distance is obtained by substituting $\mathbf{M}$ with the identity matrix. Therefore, once the user provides a set of points $\mathcal{X}$, we aim at finding a matrix $\mathbf{M}$ and a query $\boldsymbol{q}$ such that

$$\min_{\mathbf{M}, \boldsymbol{q}} (\boldsymbol{x} - \boldsymbol{q})^\top \mathbf{M}(\boldsymbol{x} - \boldsymbol{q}) \text{ subject to } \det(\mathbf{M}) = 1, \tag{6.2}$$

where the additional constraint $\det(\mathbf{M}) = 1$ avoids the trivial solution $\mathbf{M} = \mathbf{0}$.

Problem 6.2 can be efficiently solved by starting with an initial guess of the query $\boldsymbol{q_0}$ which is iteratively updated by moving the query point toward the mean of the user points. This iterative process allows online updates of MindReader, in case a new point is added to the set $\mathcal{X}$.

6.1.4   MULTI-VIEW LEARNING

An important subclass of problems for database research deals with *multi-view learning* in which different datasets or sources are used at the same time. Instead of dealing with examples x^A from a single dataset A, multi-view learning consider examples x^B from another dataset B and learns a prediction $f(y_t)$ on some combination of x^A and x^B. Multi-view learning can be seen as data integration from the machine learning perspective, and it is tightly related to transfer learning. On the same token, online multi-view learning relates to schema mapping by example presented in Section 2.3.

The methods presented so far can be adapted to multi-view learning via a majority voting approach among the different predictions [Nguyen et al., 2012]. Assume that at each iteration t an example (x^A, x^B, y_t) is retrieved, where x^A is a data item in database A and x^B is a data item in B. The prediction from the model is computed as a majority voting from the models f_{θ^A} and f_{θ^B} with parameter θ^A and θ^B, respectively,

$$\tilde{y}_t = \text{sgn}\left(\theta^A x^A + \theta^B x^B\right).$$

The parameters are learned using the hinge loss $L(y_t) = \max(0, 1 - y_t \cdot \tilde{y}_t)$ and updated in an online fashion.

6.2   ACTIVE LEARNING

We now turn our attention to algorithms that select items from a dataset to be rated by the user. In active learning, the system interactively queries the user on single data points labels. This paradigm is especially crucial for example-based approaches in which the user provides only a single initial example rather than a set of relevant examples as in the case of passive learning. In active learning, the algorithm has access to all data points upfront but not their labels, and the goal is to learn how to label those points by querying the user the minimum number of times. Therefore, referring to Algorithm 6.10, in active learning at each iteration t, instead of receiving an input from the user (Line 3), the system independently samples an element from the database and presents it to the user to obtain the label.

An active learning algorithm aims at minimizing the user's queries while maximizing the model's knowledge. As such, the sampling strategy should strike a balance between *exploration* of unknown values to improve its model and *exploitation* of that model to collect high-quality items. Quality is measure in terms of regret, which is the deviation of the loss of the model from the optimal strategy at the end of the interaction.

$$R_T = \sum_{i=1}^{T} L_t(\theta_t) - \min_{\theta} \sum_{i=1}^{T} L_t(\theta). \tag{6.3}$$

We present selected works in active learning which better fit the example-based paradigm. We first introduce the multi-armed bandits framework, which can be used to instantiate problems with the exploration-exploitation dilemma and some application of such a framework. We then present the explore-by-example framework for scalable active learning on large datasets. We conclude with an overview of other active learning methods. For a more extensive survey on the topic, we refer to the book of Settles [2012].

6.2.1 MULTI-ARMED BANDITS

Multi-armed bandits is a statistical framework for learning in the presence of partial feedback. Such a framework is useful to formulate a number of problems in active learning, as well as in the analysis of approximations in stochastic settings.

The problem is formulated as a game in which a player wants to maximize the expected reward with k slot machines. The player needs to address the tradeoff between exploration and exploitation and finding the best strategy to maximize the revenue.

Formally, the *stochastic multi-armed bandit* game takes place in T rounds. At each iteration t, the player decides to pull arm $I_t \in \{1, ..., k\}$. Each arm is associated with a probability distribution P_i with expected value μ_i. The reward $X_{i,t}$ at iteration t for arm i is drawn from the distribution P_i, $X_{i,t} \sim P_i$. Let $N_{i,n} = \sum_{t=1}^{s} \mathbb{I}\{I_t = i\}$ denote the number of times the arms i has been pulled after s iterations. Question is: which arm to we pull next?

The expected reward at the end of the iteration T is

$$
\begin{aligned}
R_T &= \max_{i=1,...,k} \mathbb{E}\left[\sum_{t=1}^{T} X_{i,t}\right] - \mathbb{E}\left[\sum_{t=1}^{T} X_{I_t,t}\right] \\
&= \max_{i=1,...,k} T\mu_i - \sum_{i=1}^{k} N_{i,T}\mu_i \\
&= T\mu_i^* - \sum_{i=1}^{k} N_{i,T}\mu_i \qquad\qquad \text{where } \mu_i^* = \max_{i=1,...,k} \mu_i \\
&= \sum_{i \neq i^*} N_{i,T}\Delta_i \qquad\qquad\qquad\quad \Delta_i = \mu_i^* - \mu_i.
\end{aligned}
$$

Therefore, we can study greedy choices that minimize the deviation Δ_i among the optimal by considering suboptimal arms $i \neq i^*$.

Upper Confidence Bound

The most common algorithm for solving the stochastic multi-armed bandits dilemma is the Upper Confidence Bound (UCB) algorithm [Auer et al., 2002]. The algorithm is based on the principle of *optimism in the face of uncertainty*: Whenever we are uncertain about the outcome of an arm, we consider the best possible world and choose the best arm. As such, the unknown reward payoff is as large as plausibly possible based on the data observed so far. Intuitively, this principle works because if the learner acting optimistically chooses the right arm than the choice is also optimal. On the other hand, if the arm is not likely to give the maximum reward, the learner will learn the actual payoff and will act accordingly in the future. This argument does not provide a convincing explanation of why a strategy designed with optimism in the face of uncertainty is a good strategy.

Plausibly best. To select the plausibly best arm, we need to define the plausibility in probabilistic terms. This concept is related to confidence intervals and best search methods which design and exploit upper bounds on some quality measure.

Recall that if $X_1, X_2, \ldots, X_n$ are independent and 1-subgaussian (i.e., $\mathbb{E}[X_i] = 0$) and $\hat{\mu} = \sum_{t=1}^{n} X_t / n$, then

$$P(\hat{\mu} \geq \epsilon) \leq \exp\left(-n\epsilon^2/2\right).$$

Equating $\exp\left(-n\epsilon^2/2\right) = \delta$ and solving with ϵ leads to

$$P\left(\hat{\mu} \geq \sqrt{\frac{2}{n} \log\left(\frac{1}{\delta}\right)}\right) \leq \delta. \tag{6.4}$$

Hence, the best plausible estimate at iteration t for arm i, given the observed samples $N_{i,t-1}$ with empirical mean reward $\hat{\mu}_{i,t-1}$, can be

$$\hat{\mu}_{i,t-1} + \sqrt{\frac{2}{N_{i,t-1}} \log\left(\frac{1}{\delta}\right)}. \tag{6.5}$$

The UCB method pulls the arm i which maximizes the quantity in Equation (6.5). If δ is chosen very small, then the algorithm will be more optimistic, and if δ is large, then the optimism is less certain. The value $1 - \delta$ is called the confidence level, and it is usually chosen to be time dependent. A common choice for that is $1/\delta = \phi(t) = 1 + t \log^2(t), t = 1, 2, \ldots$. The different UCB algorithm differs in the function ϕ and the subsequent analysis. Algorithm 6.11 describes the UCB algorithm.

Algorithm 6.11 UCB

Input: Number of arms k, number of iterations $T \geq k$, function ϕ

1: Initialize $\alpha > 0, \hat{\mu}_{i,0} \leftarrow 0, N_{i,0} \leftarrow 0$
2: **for** $t = 1, 2, \ldots, T$ **do**
3:    $I_t \leftarrow \text{argmax}_{i=1,\ldots,k} \left[\hat{\mu}_{i,t-1} + \sqrt{\frac{2\log(\phi(t))}{N_{i,t-1}}}\right]$ ▷ Choose arm to pull (Eq. 6.5)
4:    Draw $X_{I_t,t} \sim P_{I_t}$
5:    $\hat{\mu}_{I_t,t} \leftarrow \frac{N_{I_t,t-1}}{N_{I_t,t-1}+1} \hat{\mu}_{I_t,t} + \frac{1}{N_{I_t,t-1}+1} X_{I_t,t}$ ▷ Update empirical mean
6:    $N_{I_t,t} \leftarrow N_{I_t,t-1} + 1$ ▷ Update pull count
7: **end for**

As the value in Line 3 is undefined for $N_{i,t-1} = 0$ a possible choice is to fix it to t and let the player pull each arm once at the beginning. Intuitively, the bound states that if we pull a certain arm a sufficient amount of time, this will reduce the uncertainty about the arm (note the $N_{i,t-1}$ at the denominator). However, this does not mean that overall we have found a good strategy since the uncertainty on other arms will be higher. As such, the UCB in Equation (6.5) will choose arms where the confidence interval is large. Thus, the uncertainty is high. Such an algorithm leads to the following bound even in the case UCB fails, in which case the choice of ϕ is critical to ensure a sublinear regret.

Theorem 6.1   UCB Regret.   *The regret of UCB is bounded by*

$$R_n \leq \sum_{i:\Delta_i>0} \inf_{\epsilon \in (0,\Delta_i)} \Delta_i \left(1 + \frac{5}{\epsilon^2} + \frac{2}{(\Delta_i - \epsilon)^2} \left(\log \phi(n) + \sqrt{\pi \log \phi(n)} + 1 \right) \right). \qquad (6.6)$$

Furthermore,

$$\limsup_{n \to \infty} R_n / \log(n) \leq \sum_{i:\Delta_i>0} \frac{2}{\Delta_i}. \qquad (6.7)$$

Therefore, the regret slowly decreases as $\log(n)$ which justifies the choice of the function $\phi(n)$.

Contextual Bandits

One useful extension to the multi-armed bandits setting is the one in which the number of arms is large, but every arm is associated with contextual information. This extension, called *contextual bandits* [Li et al., 2010], shines in recommendation scenarios where many products are available, and the user makes informed choices based on the context.

In contextual bandits, the state of the environment, such as query logs or preferences from the user, are taken into account. This generates a set of possible alternatives given the current state of the environment or the knowledge gathered so far. These alternatives are called policies $\mathcal{F}$. Each policy associates a context $x \in \mathcal{X} \subseteq \mathbb{R}^n$ to an arm i. The regret is then defined on the the decision I_t with the best policy $f^* = \arg\inf_{f \in \mathcal{F}} L(f)$:

$$R_T(f) = \sum_{t=1}^{T} L_{I_t,t} - L_t \left(f^* \right).$$

The LinUCB [Li et al., 2010] is an extension of UCB for solving the contextual bandits problem.

6.2.2   GAUSSIAN PROCESSES

Multi-armed bandits assume independence among the arms. However, independent arms perform poorly in scenarios in which the knowledge of one item provides information on other items. Also, the reward obtained by pulling an arm is usually noisy. Consider for instance the case in which the user provides ratings for products. A user's rating is influenced by many factors, such as the mood or the moment. As such, the *utility* of the evaluation is inherently noisy.

We present a particularly useful model, Gaussian Processes (see Rasmussen [2004] for a complete book), which is connected to multi-armed bandits, designs of experiments, and Bayesian optimization. Gaussian processes fall into the category of nonparametric models as the model parameters are, by definition, infinite and increase with the number of observations.

Definition 6.2 Gaussian Process.   Formally, a function f is a Gaussian Process (GP) $f \sim \mathcal{N}(\mu, \mathbf{K})$ if any finite set of values $f(x_1), \ldots, f(x_n)$ has a multivariate normal distribution, where the inputs x_n are typically vectors from any space. A GP is specified by a mean function $\mu(x)$ and a covariance function $k(x, x')$, otherwise known as a kernel that forms the covariance matrix $\mathbf{K} = [k(i, j)]_{i=1}^n$. That is, for any $x, x', \mu(x) = \mathbb{E}[f(x)]$ and $k(x, x') = \text{Cov}(f(x), f(x'))$.

The shape and smoothness of our function are determined by the covariance function, as it controls the correlation between all pairs of output values. Thus, if $k(x, x')$ is large when x and x' are near one another, the function will be more smooth, while smaller kernel values imply a more jagged function. More intuitively, a Gaussian Process is a distribution over functions, as the number of points is infinite, sampled from a Gaussian distribution, and entirely determined by the covariance matrix.

GP is a Bayesian method, hence learning begins with a prior (Normal in this case) distribution and updates this as data points are observed, producing the posterior distribution over functions. When a data point is observed from the user, the posterior is computed from the prior. Figure 6.2 shows an example of a Gaussian Process prior and prediction on the (unknown) dotted function $f(x) = x \sin(x)$, the dots represent the user's evaluations (x, y), the line the GP's mean, the shadowed area the 95% confidence interval (variance). The confidence intervals are narrower than other regions next to the observed points.

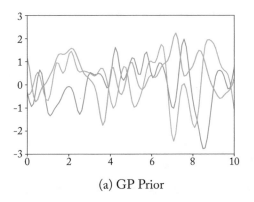
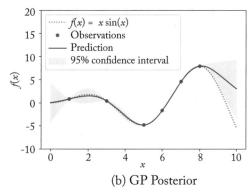

(a) GP Prior

(b) GP Posterior

Figure 6.2: Gaussian Process prior and posterior for for function $f(x) = x \sin(x)$.

A critical property of GPs is the incremental updates of the model parameters μ and $\mathbf{K}$ without recomputing the entire covariance matrix. Note that, as explained in Bishop et al. [2006], the prediction of the value of a new object $\mathbf{x}$ involves the inversion of the covariance matrix, which is $\mathcal{O}(n^3)$ where n is the number of observations. However, approximate methods can boost the actual performance and avoid the expensive matrix inversion [Gonzalez and Hong, 2008, Wainwright et al., 2001].

More recently, advances in neural network have resorted in modeling distributions over functions with neural networks. These Conditional Neural Processes (CNPs) [Garnelo et al., 2018] capture arbitrary conditional distributions of the predictions over the data, while generalizing the family of functions that can be learned by a traditional GP. The advantages of encoding distributions into neural networks lay in the lower complexity of learning and the modeling power of such CNPs.

Upper Confidence Bounds for Gaussian Processes
Gaussian processes and multi-armed bandits are closely related since in both cases we are sampling from an unknown distribution and each step we receive a reward. The connection has been established by Srinivas et al. [2010], where a UCB algorithm for Gaussian Processes is proposed. The purpose is to select input examples from the data, such that the regret is bounded by the number of iterations. Given an unknown function $f : \mathbb{R}^n \rightarrow \mathbb{R}$ and a sequence of observations $\mathbf{x}_1, ..., \mathbf{x}_T$ the goal is minimizing

$$R_T = \sum_{i=1}^{T} \left[f\left(\mathbf{x}_{opt}\right) - f\left(\mathbf{x}_i\right) \right]. \tag{6.8}$$

Ideally, the observations are picked in way that $\frac{1/T}{R_T} \rightarrow 0$ as $T \rightarrow +\infty$ converges fast.

GP-UCB is a greedy algorithm with quality guarantees on the regret for an unknown function modeled as a Gaussian Process $f \sim GP(0, k(\mathbf{x}, \mathbf{x}'))$ where k is a covariance function or kernel. At each step t the algorithm selects

$$\mathbf{x}_t = \operatorname*{argmax}_{\mathbf{x}} \underbrace{\mu_{t-1}(\mathbf{x})}_{\text{Exploitation}} + \underbrace{\sqrt{\beta_t}\sigma_{t-1}(\mathbf{x})}_{\text{Exploration}} \tag{6.9}$$

and observes

$$y_t = f(\mathbf{x}_t) + \epsilon_t,$$

where $\epsilon \sim \mathcal{N}(0, \sigma^2 \mathbf{I})$ is the noise in the observations (e.g., user's errors, sensor's imprecisions). Equation (6.9) provides a trade-off between exploration by sampling on high uncertain points $\sigma_{t-1}(\mathbf{x})$, and exploitation by sampling close to the predicted values $\mu_{t-1}(\mathbf{x})$. The value β_t is chosen as $\beta_t = \mathcal{O}(\log t)$ in a way that the more the samples, the lower the uncertainty. The following theorem provides the relation among regret and the choice of β_t.

Theorem 6.3 *If at step t we choose $\beta_t = \mathcal{O}(\log t)$, then with high probability*

$$R_T = \mathcal{O}\left(T\sqrt{\frac{\gamma_T}{T}}\right),$$

where $\gamma_T = \max_{|A|\leq T} I(f; y_A)$ is the maximum information gain due to sampling.

An extension of GP-UCB for high-dimensional data [Djolonga et al., 2013]

Active Search with GP-Select

Active search [Garnett et al., 2012] tries to unveil as many elements of a particular class as possible. GP-Select is an active search algorithm that employs GP-UCB [Srinivas et al., 2010] for classification until a specific budget is depleted. Each element in the database $x \in \mathbf{D}$ is associated with a cost $c(x)$. The value of an element is an unknown function f. For any subset of the database $S \subseteq \mathbf{D}$, the utility $F(S)$ of the set is the sum of the values $F(S) = \sum_{x\in S} f(x)$. Given a budget Λ the goal is to return the set S^* such that

$$S^* = \operatorname*{argmax}_{\sum_{x\in S} c(x)\leq\Lambda} F(S). \tag{6.10}$$

The approximate solution for this problem models the value function f as a Gaussian Process and applies the GP-UCB algorithm to select new elements to evaluate. GP-Select algorithm is shown in Algorithm 6.12.

Algorithm 6.12 GP-Select

Input: Database $\mathbf{D}$, kernel k, budget Λ
1: $S \leftarrow \emptyset$
2: **for** $t = 1, 2, ..., \Lambda$ **do**
3:     $\mu_{t-1}, \sigma^2_{t-1} \leftarrow$ GP-Inference$(k, (S, y_{t-1}))$ ▷ Model update
4:     $x_t \leftarrow \operatorname{argmax}_{x\in\mathbf{D}} \mu_{t-1}(x) + \sqrt{\beta_t}\sigma_{t-1}(x)$ ▷ Item selection
5:     $S \leftarrow S \cup \{x_t\}$
6:     Get feedback $y_t \leftarrow f(x) + \epsilon_t$
7: **end for**

Active Search in Graphs

Ma et al. [2015] proposes GP-SOPT, an active search for graph data. The idea is to extend the previous work of Srinivas et al. [2010] to include prior knowledge about the graph structure. The main differences between GP-UCP and GP-Select are in the node selection strategy and the prior which is computed on the adjacency matrix of the graph.

In GP-SOPT, we are given a graph $G : \langle V, E \rangle$, with nodes V and edges $E \subseteq V \times V$. The *adjacency matrix* $\mathbf{A}$ of G is a matrix with elements $\mathbf{A}_{ij} = 1$ if $(i, j) \in E$ and $\mathbf{A}_{ij} = 0$ otherwise. The *Laplacian matrix* is $\mathbf{L} = \mathbf{D} - \mathbf{A}$ where $\mathbf{D}$ is a diagonal matrix having the degree of node i at $\mathbf{D}_{ii} = \sum_{j=1}^{|V|} \mathbf{A}_{ij}$. The unknown value $f(x)$ of each node $v \in V$ has prior

$$f \sim \mathcal{N}\left(\mu_0 \mathbf{1}, \mathbf{L}^{-1} = (\mathbf{D} - \mathbf{A} + \omega_0 \mathbf{I})^{-1}\right).$$

Differently from GP-Select, a new node is selected using Σ-optimality criteria [Ma et al., 2013] which bring better regret guarantees than UCB. Figure 6.3 shows a visual comparison between UCB and GP-Select.

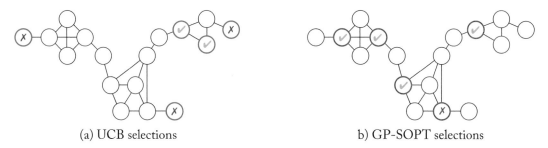

(a) UCB selections   b) GP-SOPT selections

Figure 6.3: Comparison between UCB node selection (a) and GP-SOPT node selection (b) on a small graph. GP-SOPT selects nodes from different communities using Σ-optimality criterion.

6.3   EXPLORE-BY-EXAMPLE

Active learning strategies normally require to check all data points to perform optimal strategies. However, in database applications when real-time responses and scalability are issues, such an approach is unsustainable. Explore-by-example (AIDE) [Dimitriadou et al., 2014, 2016] proposes a solution which samples from different areas of the data and returns the user's areas of interest using disjunctions or conjunctions of (range) queries. As such, AIDE supports the user in query formulation without in an interactive and example-based way. The AIDE framework is represented in Figure 6.4.

The first step in the AIDE framework is the partition of the data space into areas in which samples are generated and proposed to the user. The user then marks relevant and irrelevant samples, and a classifier is trained with them. Since the classification results should be interpretable, a decision tree is trained. Decision trees partition the space into orthogonal subspaces which can be interpreted as rules or queries. The misclassified samples are then used as a new center point for sampling areas. AIDE, using a simple classifier and partition method, can scale on the large dataset; however, the number of required samples to obtain a good accuracy is in the order of hundreds.

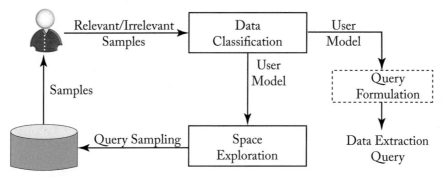

Figure 6.4: The AIDE framework.

Challenges and Future Directions: Online learning approaches conveniently integrate knowledge from the data to knowledge from the user enabling example-based exploration. However, up to now such approaches have been only partially harnessed for exploratory purposes. Moreover, scalability and fast convergence is still an issue, as the number of requests to the user (or any Oracle) is in the order of hundreds, which is not practical in an online scenario. An exciting direction to look at is the integration of knowledge from peer users [Murugesan and Carbonell, 2017] or external, cheaper sources as query logs or similarities [Kandasamy et al., 2016]. On the scalability side, machine learning approaches can benefit from advances in GPU and hardware as well as linear algebra [Hernández-Lobato and Hernández-Lobato, 2016]. Last, machine learning methods could be used to construct adaptive indexes on various kind of data [Kraska et al., 2018] intelligently.

CHAPTER 7

The Road Ahead

Exploratory search is the process of investigating an unfamiliar domain. As mentioned at the beginning of this book, in recent years, we have witnessed a growing importance of exploratory search. We produce data at unprecedented scale and speed and in heterogeneous and unco-ordinated ways. This deluge of information renders the understanding of the dataset at hand a cumbersome activity by itself. Exploratory search describes the activity of a user that tries to identify and make sense of the portion of the data that is relevant within an overwhelming search space.

The use of examples can ease data exploration by reducing the need for complex queries and expertise in the data-analytics tools, effectively simplifying the task of specifying *the information need*. Exemplar queries minimize (and in some cases eliminate) the need to understand the schema of the dataset, and they allow for some uncertainty in the search conditions. We have seen how different studies provide example-based search paradigms for structured and un-structured data. Such solutions are key-ingredients for exploratory search systems, necessary but not sufficient. The work to be done, now, is to build fully featured search systems that support exploratory search activities during their entire life-cycle.

In this chapter, we outline the main research directions toward which we envision new research efforts for the design and development of exploratory search systems. These research directions stem naturally from recent development in complementary research areas. First, we look back at the road paved since the initial overview presented by White and Roth [2009] that surveyed the exploratory search-task. In their work they list a set of features necessary to support exploratory search activities.

Features of Exploratory Search Systems [White and Roth, 2009]:

1. **Support querying and rapid query refinement:** Systems must help users formulate queries and adjust queries and views on search results in real time.

2. **Offer facets and metadata-based result filtering:** Systems must allow users to explore and filter results through the selection of facets and document metadata.

3. **Leverage search context:** Systems must leverage available information about their user, their situation, and the current exploratory search task.

4. **Offer visualizations to support insight and decision making:** Systems must present customizable visual representations of the collection being explored to support hypothesis generation and trend spotting.

5. **Support learning and understanding:** Systems must help users acquire both knowledge and skills by presenting information in ways amenable to learning given the user's current knowledge/skill level.

6. **Facilitate collaboration:** Systems must facilitate synchronous and asynchronous collaboration between users in support of task division and knowledge sharing.

7. **Offer histories, workspaces, and progress updates:** Systems must allow users to backtrack quickly, store and manipulate useful information fragments, and provide updates of progress toward an information goal.

8. **Support task management:** Systems must allow users to store, retrieve, and share search tasks in support of multisession and multiuser exploratory search scenarios.

In this categorization, example-based query paradigms address the first point, i.e., they support querying, especially for non-expert users. Yet, examples may be ambiguous, and the system may have a hard time in generalizing the search conditions that apply to the results. From this, two other features follow as complementary, the metadata-based result filtering, and the leveraging of search context. These two points are to be implemented via *interactivity* and *personalization*. Note that the two are tightly connected: during interaction with the user, the system can improve and learn more about the user needs, henceforth, enabling better personalization. Hence, the first research direction we envision regards **techniques to support interactive and personalized example-based explorations.** Furthermore, while example-based query paradigms facilitate query specification, this does not provide any help to the user trying to make sense of the result-set retrieved as an answer. For instance, the user needs to understand how the items retrieved relate to the examples provided. It follows the need for *explanations, visualization, and summarization* that help users understand and distill knowledge out of the results of their search, which is in agreement with the fourth and fifth feature identified by White and Roth [2009]. Consequently, the second research direction that we anticipate would attract further studies refers to **example-driven visualizations, summarizations, and explanations, paired with methods to suggest further example-based explorations**. Finally, some new challenges and opportunities are connected with the variety of data models and data-producing applications existing nowadays, and with the need for enabling access to this data to a broader, non-technical, audience.

7.1   SUPPORTING INTERACTIVE EXPLORATIONS

Exploration entails a dynamic process, not a one-shot query-answer interaction. The user starts from a known point in the data-space, surveys the surroundings, gains a new understanding, and based on this formulates a more precise or even wholly different query to retrieve the desired information and iterate again. During this process, the information need may evolve, or new information needs may arise. Many works have studied how to support this dynamic process, Idreos et al. [2015] surveyed some of these works, and others we have analyzed in the previous chapters. In particular, the Queriosity data exploration system [Wasay et al., 2015] envisions an evolution of this trend toward a proactive system that *"engages the user to answer current questions and exposes future exploration directions."*

We identify four main steps in an interactive exploration (illustrated in the rounded boxes of Figure 7.1), namely: (i) query processing, (ii) results analysis, (iii) results presentation, and (iv) generation of exploration alternatives. In the following, we describe future research directions for each of them.

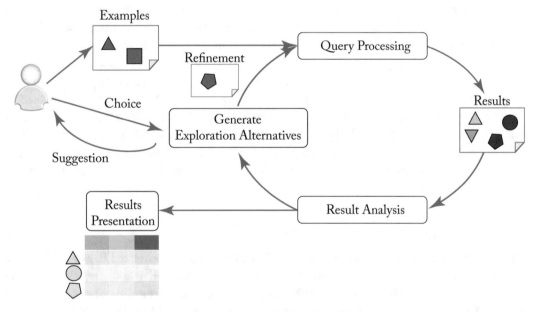

Figure 7.1: Interactive process supporting Exploration-by-Example.

7.1.1   QUERY PROCESSING

Query processing is the core part of a search system. In an interactive exploratory workflow, multiple queries run one after the other as the user proceeds with the exploration. This calls for fast and scalable query execution systems that take advantage of modern hardware and can easily adapt to new hardware architectures, such as the Spartex framework, developed by Abdelaziz et al. [2017]. Another critical characteristic of exploratory queries is that they are often very similar one to the other, or they touch a similar portion of the data. That is because with each query the user learns some new information that is used to refine the query itself and inform the following one. Often, in this process, the results of each intermediate query are quickly thrown away after just a quick look. If a system presents data while still processing a query, this means that many queries will be interrupted before they could terminate their computation.

These two insights highlight the importance of **fast query processing** on the one hand, and the opportunity to **avoid the full recomputation of a query** (by exploiting the result of previous queries) on the other hand. Moreover, the system could **limit the computation to only a sample** of the result-set that is informative, instead of wasting resources on computing a complete answer that will not be consumed (see, for instance, the NeedleTail system by Kim et al. [2018]). In this direction, Wasay et al. [2017] propose to store some precomputed results in cache-like data-structures, those results are primitive aggregates that can be composed to estimate the results of more complex queries. We also envision the need of **adaptive query executions** (similar in spirit to what was proposed, for a different case, by Kohn et al. [2018]), where the system can independently decide to approximate, sample, or avoid the execution of some queries or parts of them. On the same token, the integration with **adaptive data-structures and indexes**, similar to the approach proposed by Idreos et al. [2007] with database cracking, and by Zoumpatianos et al. [2016] adaptive incremental indexing, are of crucial importance in providing the necessary performance. Among those techniques, a recent exciting research direction is described by Idreos et al. [2018] with their proposal of a "Data Calculator," which enables interactive and semi-automated design of data structures based on workload and hardware. This would allow, for instance, a system to adapt its internal data structures and processing to the specific data-access requirements of the explorer's information needs on the dataset at hand.

7.1.2   AUTOMATIC RESULT ANALYSIS

Automatic data analysis is a necessary functionality that is tightly connected to any exploratory information need. The exploration system should help the user understand the results of the query, in order to cope with a vague user's information need and uncertainty about the content of the database. Such vagueness calls for systems that **automatically identify peculiar characteristics, possible trends, anomalies, and outliers**. On the one hand, this enables an *appropriate presentation* (visualization) of the results; on the other hand, this step will help the user understand whether they found the desired information and otherwise lead to the generation of different exploration paths. To address this task we not only require the system to identify the characteristic features of the result-set but also to describe how they relate with other portions of the dataset as well. One extreme case, for instance, is the so-called *empty answer problem*, i.e., the case of an empty (or maybe exceptionally small) result-set. In this case, the causes of this (probably unexpected) outcome should be identified in the query and the data and communicated to the user to help them reformulate their query.

More often, as a result of an ambiguous or under-specified query, the resultset will be too large to be processed by the user. This calls both for **data-summarization techniques and for automatic discovery of insights**. As anticipated earlier, Queriosity [Wasay et al., 2015] envisions such functionalities. Furthermore, Tang et al. [2017] tackle in practice the problem of automatically extracting top-k insights from multi-dimensional data. Similarly, MacroBase [Bailis et al., 2017] can analyze large data-series and not only quickly identify outliers, but can also summarize and describe commonalities among points in a class, as well as differences between classes, helping in this way the analyst in detecting important patterns in the data. These works, all point to the design of a system that can *autonomously* identify what is interesting within a dataset. Yet, the existing solutions are in their infancy and limited in the type of data and the insights they support.

7.2 PRESENTING ANSWERS AND EXPLORATION ALTERNATIVES

As soon as the exploration starts and the system produces some answer, the user ought to understand whether these answers fit their information need. In this case, information overload might be a problem in large datasets, since an ambiguous query is likely to produce a large result-set. Hence, summarizing the results is extremely important for the answer to be *consumable* and *informative*. One of the most effective ways to summarize and present data to a user is to employ some visualization technique, e.g., charts, maps, and hierarchies. Yet, it is hard for non-expert users to generate such visualizations manually. Research is focusing on navigation systems that automaticaly support the user in this task. Given the iterative nature of explorations, the system should help the user understanding in which direction the exploration can proceed. That is, it should suggest query reformulations, and help with query refinements.

7.2.1 RESULTS PRESENTATION

Information visualization allows users to understand the salient characteristics of a set of datapoints easily. Visualization allows identifying trends, anomalies, and outliers. Visualization techniques and systems have received much attention in the past decades, and more recently they have been complemented with tools to help in visual query-specification (see, for instance, the works by Pienta et al. [2015, 2017], and Song et al. [2018]). We refer the reader to the lectures by Tominski [2015], and by Scholtz [2017] for a broader view of data visualization techniques. We highlight here the recent trends in the **automatic discovery of insights** and how they naturally complement **automatic visualization recommendation techniques**. In this context, the works by Siddiqui et al. [2016], Vartak et al. [2017], and Luo et al. [2018] identify what is interesting in the data, how to best present this with a visual representation, and ultimately guide the user in the search for the desired visual patterns. The inclusion of these techniques in any exploration system is a first necessary step for a general purpose exploration system. Moreover, researchers are already studying how **to use examples to identify the data visualizations that are more interesting for the user**. In the context of example-driven data-exploration, data visualizations should provide support to the user and select examples and refinements for exploratory queries.

Summaries are also handy when dealing with a significant amount of data. A summary distills a concise representation of the contents of a large dataset by aggregating measures along the salient dimensions of the objects. In particular, summaries have been proved useful both for large high-dimensional datasets and for datasets with very complex structures (e.g., graphs). In particular, works by Čebirić et al. [2015] and Song et al. [2016] exploited graph-summaries to improve query performances of graph queries. Here, we envision **the use of data-summarization techniques to represent the large result-set of an exploratory query**. **Approximate query processing** is yet another flexible mechanism that combines summaries with probabilistic models of the content of a dataset to provide approximate answers. As mentioned earlier, in exploratory settings, the user can accept some imprecision in the answer-set retrieved as long as it preserves the possibility to extract the correct insights. Orr et al. [2017], for instance, present a system that can provide fast query-response capabilities, faster than sampling, while introducing the same amount of uncertainty (or errors). These methods can be guided by user-provided examples that can inform the summarization system on which aspect to favor. At the same time, precomputed summaries for portions of the datasets can be matched against the user examples, and be in this way exploited for identifying the desired answers.

7.2.2   GENERATION OF EXPLORATION ALTERNATIVES

As we said earlier, an open-ended information need often starts from an ambiguous, possibly underspecified, query. The interaction with the system guides the refinement of the query and of the information need itself. In this process, the system cannot remain passive, blindly executing each query and leaving the user on its own. Similar to the case for automatic insight discovery and presentation, **the system should also suggest to the user how to reformulate the original query** (e.g., how to enrich the provided examples, or which examples to add and remove), and along which dimension the next query could be filtered or expanded. For instance, Chatzopoulou et al. [2009] propose a query recommender system for relational databases based on the paradigm of collaborative filtering and on a log of relational queries. Given the current query, such a system suggests a set of related queries to help undecided users. Yet, the query recommendation technique devised by Chatzopoulou et al. [2009] is limited to the history of previous interactions of other users with the system.

By exploiting data summarization techniques, we can **identify related queries by exploring the query-space** and rely only on the information extracted from the database. Data-driven exploration is the idea pitched in Charles [Sellam et al., 2013], a *query advisory system*. The intuition behind Charles is to infer queries from data. Hence, the system may infer possible relevant queries from the whole database, but also from the result of a previous query. This is similar to the concept of *faceted search* (see for instance the work by Roy et al. [2009]). In a faceted search-system, only a few significant results are returned, while in a separate area, the system displays several attributes that characterize the answers (e.g., when searching for products, these may be brand, price, and size). These attributes are the facets, and for each of the several attribute values, ranges are proposed; by selecting one or more of those ranges, the user can refine the selection. We expect similar techniques to apply to an example-based search system, where different facets are related to representative examples.

To support interactive data exploration, similarly to the Charles system mentioned earlier and to Queriosity, Papaemmanouil et al. [2016] also promote a system-aided exploration of big data spaces. In this vision, a critical aspect is the ability of the system to **learn user interests automatically** and infer the queries that retrieve data relevant to the user interests. These systems exploit interactive learning approaches to prompt the user with questions requesting their feedback on specific data samples (as presented in Chapter 6). Yet, there is still much work to do for extending these methods to more complex search spaces (e.g., graphs) and to expand the range of supported queries and operations (from simple aggregation queries, to more complex analytical queries). Moreover, when many exploration alternatives can be provided to the user, the system should (once more) exploit information about user preferences and the user goal to decide which options to present first.

> **Tools for advanced Data Exploration:** Data exploration is a dynamic and interactive process. The nature of the process requires the system to be **adaptive** and **responsive**. The system should *adapt to the user need*. To this end, exploratory methods should employ **user models** and **specialized machine learning techniques** to reach adaptability and personalization.
>
> At the same time, the system should be able to respond to user queries and provide timely response swiftly; this may be at the expense of accuracy as long as the answers retrieved can still provide the required insights. As exploratory systems are commonly employed with large databases, the **scalability** of algorithms should be a first-class citizen. **Approximate methods** could be employed, especially when faced with large datasets, to assure reasonable response time.

7.3   NEW CHALLENGES

Looking at the most recent developments in the fields of data management, data integration, and data mining, we see many important factors in the development of new exploratory search systems. These factors include the need of businesses and organizations to deal with and integrate data of multiple different types, the need above to customize the experience for every single user, the trend to allow access to data to non-expert users in everyday use cases, and finally the advancement in new human-computer interfaces.

7.3.1   EXPLORE HETEROGENEOUS DATA

In the previous chapters, we surveyed methods for example-based search in different data-models. All the solutions we presented adapt to a single data model, either relational data, graphs, or documents. Even so, in many situations, **complementary information is stored in distinct repositories and with different data formats**. For this reason, data analysts often need to combine information from many heterogeneous datasets. The next steps in data-exploration system development should embrace this heterogeneity, both in data and in query workloads. In particular, Karpathiotakis et al. [2016] make a case for a system able to query data in different formats, in their case an analytical query engine that queries CSV, JSON, and relational data. The Myria Big Data Management [Halperin et al., 2014] is also a federated data management and analytics system with a query execution engine that can query different backend engines with different data models. A search engine as such is a polystore architecture since specific data-models are handled separately by different systems. Finally, Chirigati et al. [2016] focus on a different aspect, that is to integrate and correlated information from distinct datasets generated by different sources. In their case, they focus on spatiotemporal datasets. In particular, they introduce the concept of *Data Polygamy*. The goal is to find all data-sets related to a given data set: two data-sets are related if there exists a relationship between some spatiotemporal regions that exhibit unusual behaviors.

The recent works seem to suggest that exploratory systems cannot settle on a single dataset and data-model, but they need to embrace different datasets, storing data with different data models, stored in different systems. Moreover, the exploration should encompass examples presented in different formats, and discover the implicit relationships across models automatically.

7.3.2   PERSONALIZED EXPLORATIONS

Personalizing search results has a long history (see, for instance, Jeh and Widom [2003], Vallet and Castells [2012], and Chakrabarti [2007]), similarly personalized query suggestions have also been studied extensively (e.g., Teevan et al. [2005] and Shokouhi [2013]). Also, some traditional data-mining techniques have been extended in order to incorporate user-preferences (see the work by Perozzi et al. [2014] in Chapter 3, Garrigós et al. [2009] on personalized OLAP, or Preti et al. [2018] on weighted pattern mining). Earlier we discussed also the importance of exploiting contextual information and user preferences (inferred from previous interactions); those arguments are intrinsic in the concept of personalized search. Systems able to exploit query-logs, user profiles, prior searches, and user context to guide exploratory search are still in their infancy. Exploiting user preferences is an essential area with new horizons to be explored, in particular given the fact that new use-cases and new users are getting into play.

7.3.3 EXPLORATION FOR EVERYBODY

The main advantage of the example-based query paradigms is to prevent inexperienced users from formulating queries using a complex query language. As such, domain expert but not necessary database expert can access the desired information with little effort. Furthermore, exploration practices help non-expert users to extract knowledge from complex datasets. The welcomed result is that involved exploration tasks, and complex datasets are becoming appealing for and accessible to an ever-growing audience.

Example-based exploration completes the paradigm shift of the so-called *Big Data* from data experts to data consumers. One of the elements that lead to the Big Data era is the fact that every person became a data-producer thank to the web, the social media, and personal devices. Now, the final step is for every user to be able to tap into this stream of data and become a data-consumer. This shift requires tools that are easy to use (we can think of graphical interfaces), but also that work on commodity hardware (e.g., mobile devices), and that can assist with tasks that are useful for the common use-cases. In this direction we see the convergence of new studies on user friendly visual query systems (e.g., X2Q [Lissandrini et al., 2018a], or Sapphire [El-Roby et al., 2016]), mobile cloud computing techniques (see the survey by Dinh et al. [2013]), and new interaction methods, like natural language interfaces (e.g., Li and Jagadish [2016] for relational databases) and new devices (e.g., motion capture-based device like Kinect and HoloLens, as described by O'hara et al. [2013] and Jiang and Nandi [2015]).

CHAPTER 8

Conclusions

Exploratory methods are a bridge between the vagueness of the user need and the complexity of the data. On the road toward usability, such methods provide a fresh perspective, in which the user is the first-class citizen in the discovery of new information. A more democratic process to data understanding and use include non-expert users, which cannot formulate complex search queries to find the required information.

This book has presented example-based exploratory methods as a fresh ground for research that shifts the traditional view from queries to examples. In such methods, the user query is an example of the intended results. We have surveyed the representative work in this area on relational, graphs, and textual data models. The book comprehensively covers different aspects and provides easy taxonomies and new insights to help the creation of an exploratory system, as well as fostering the research in this area. Moreover, we have shown how complex tasks, such as finding correspondences in the entities on different databases or retrieving communities of nodes, can be elegantly solved with an example-based approach. Example-based approaches also improve the search experience as reported in several user-studies.

As a step forward, we have shed light on challenges and exciting research involving machine learning and adaptive systems. The maturity of most of the methods calls finally for implementation of real-world example-based data exploration systems.

Bibliography

Ibrahim Abdelaziz, Razen Harbi, Semih Salihoglu, and Panos Kalnis. Combining vertex-centric graph processing with SPARQL for large-scale RDF data analytics. *IEEE Transactions on Parallel Distributed Systems*, 28(12):3374–3388, 2017. DOI: 10.1109/tpds.2017.2720174 116

Alberto Abelló, Jérôme Darmont, Lorena Etcheverry, Matteo Golfarelli, Jose-Norberto Mazón, Felix Naumann, Torben Pedersen, Stefano Bach Rizzi, Juan Trujillo, Panos Vassiliadis, et al. Fusion cubes: Towards self-service business intelligence. *IJDWM*, 9(2):66–88, 2013. DOI: 10.4018/jdwm.2013040104 95

Serge Abiteboul, Richard Hull, and Victor Vianu. *Foundations of Databases: The Logical Level*. Addison-Wesley Longman Publishing Co., Inc., 1995. 12, 13

Eugene Agichtein and Luis Gravano. Snowball: Extracting relations from large plain-text collections. In *JCDL*, pages 85–94, 2000. DOI: 10.1145/336597.336644 67, 80, 81, 87, 91

Shmuel Agmon. The relaxation method for linear inequalities. *Canadian Journal of Mathematics*, 6(3):382–392, 1954. DOI: 10.4153/cjm-1954-037-2 101

Bogdan Alexe, Balder Ten Cate, Phokion G. Kolaitis, and Wang-Chiew Tan. Characterizing schema mappings via data examples. *TODS*, 36(4):23, 2011a. DOI: 10.1145/2043652.2043656 26, 35

Bogdan Alexe, Balder Ten Cate, Phokion G. Kolaitis, and Wang-Chiew Tan. Designing and refining schema mappings via data examples. In *SIGMOD*, pages 133–144, 2011b. DOI: 10.1145/1989323.1989338 26, 35

Reid Andersen, Fan Chung, and Kevin Lang. Local graph partitioning using pagerank vectors. In *FOCS*, pages 475–486, 2006. DOI: 10.1109/focs.2006.44 49

Marcelo Arenas and Martin Ugarte. Designing a query language for RDF: Marrying open and closed worlds. *TODS*, 42(4):21:1–21:46, 2017. DOI: 10.1145/3129247 39

Marcelo Arenas, Alexandre Bertails, Eric Prud'hommeaux, and Juan Sequeda. A direct mapping of relational data to RDF. *W3C Recommendation*, 27, 2012. 90

Marcelo Arenas, Gonzalo I. Diaz, and Egor V. Kostylev. Reverse engineering SPARQL queries. In *WWW*, pages 239–249, 2016. DOI: 10.1145/2872427.2882989 39, 55, 56, 58, 64, 66

Peter Auer, Nicolo Cesa-Bianchi, and Paul Fischer. Finite-time analysis of the multiarmed bandit problem. *Machine Learning*, 47(2–3):235–256, 2002. DOI: https://doi.org/10.1023/A:1013689704352 104

Nguyen Bach and Sameer Badaskar. A review of relation extraction. *Literature Review for Language and Statistics II*, 2, 2007. 80

Peter Bailis, Edward Gan, Samuel Madden, Deepak Narayanan, Kexin Rong, and Sahaana Suri. Macrobase: Prioritizing attention in fast data. In *SIGMOD*, pages 541–556, ACM, New York, 2017. DOI: 10.1145/3035918.3035928 117

Pablo Barceló Baeza. Querying graph databases. In *PODS*, pages 175–188, 2013. DOI: 10.1145/2463664.2465216 52

Sonia Bergamaschi, Elton Domnori, Francesco Guerra, Raquel Trillo Lado, and Yannis Velegrakis. Keyword search over relational databases: A metadata approach. In *SIGMOD*, pages 565–576, 2011. DOI: 10.1145/1989323.1989383 90

Sourav S. Bhowmick, Byron Choi, and Chengkai Li. Graph querying meets HCI: State of the art and future directions. In *SIGMOD*, pages 1731–1736, 2017. DOI: 10.1145/3035918.3054774 34

Carsten Binnig, Donald Kossmann, and Eric Lo. Reverse query processing. In *ICDE*, pages 506–515, 2007a. DOI: 10.1109/icde.2007.367896 14

Carsten Binnig, Donald Kossmann, Eric Lo, and M. Tamer Özsu. Qagen: Generating query-aware test databases. In *SIGMOD*, pages 341–352, 2007b. DOI: 10.1145/1247480.1247520 14

Christopher M. Bishop, et al. *Pattern Recognition and Machine Learning*. Springer-Verlag New York, Inc., Secaucus, NJ, 2006. 108

D. M. Blei, A. Y. Ng, and M. I. Jordan. Latent Dirichlet allocation. *The Journal of Machine Learning Research*, 3, 2003. 71

Angela Bonifati, Radu Ciucanu, and Aurélien Lemay. Learning path queries on graph databases. In *EDBT*, pages 109–120, 2015. 39, 52, 53, 54, 55, 56, 64

Angela Bonifati, Radu Ciucanu, and Sławek Staworko. Learning join queries from user examples. *TODS*, 40(4):24, 2016. DOI: 10.1145/2818637 26, 35, 66

Angela Bonifati, Ugo Comignani, Emmanuel Coquery, and Romuald Thion. Interactive mapping specification with exemplar tuples. In *SIGMOD*, pages 667–682, 2017. DOI: 10.1145/3035918.3064028 27, 28

Ilaria Bordino, Gianmarco De Francisci Morales, Ingmar Weber, and Francesco Bonchi. From machu_picchu to rafting the urubamba river: Anticipating information needs via the entity-query graph. In *WSDM*, pages 275–284, 2013. DOI: 10.1145/2433396.2433433 76, 77, 78, 86, 93, 94

Kevin W. Boyack and Richard Klavans. Co-citation analysis, bibliographic coupling, and direct citation: Which citation approach represents the research front most accurately? *Journal of the Association for Information Science and Technology*, 61(12):2389–2404, 2010. DOI: 10.1002/asi.21419 76

Sergey Brin. Extracting patterns and relations from the World Wide Web. In *WebDB Worskshop, EDBT*, 1998. DOI: 10.1007/10704656_11 80

Peter Buneman, Sanjeev Khanna, Keishi Tajima, and Wang-Chiew Tan. Archiving scientific data. *TODS*, 29(1):2–42, 2004. DOI: 10.1145/974750.974752 11

Balder Ten Cate, Víctor Dalmau, and Phokion G. Kolaitis. Learning schema mappings. *TODS*, 38(4):28, 2013. DOI: 10.1145/2274576.2274596 26, 35

Šejla Čebirić, François Goasdoué, and Ioana Manolescu. Query-oriented summarization of RDF graphs. *PVLDB*, 8(12):2012–2015, 2015. DOI: 10.14778/2824032.2824124 65, 118

Nicolo Cesa-Bianchi, Alex Conconi, and Claudio Gentile. A second-order perceptron algorithm. *SIAM Journal on Computing*, 34(3):640–668, 2005. DOI: 10.1137/s0097539703432542 101

Ugur Cetintemel, Mitch Cherniack, Justin DeBrabant, Yanlei Diao, Kyriaki Dimitriadou, Alexander Kalinin, Olga Papaemmanouil, and Stanley B. Zdonik. Query steering for interactive data exploration. In *CIDR*, 2013. 3

Soumen Chakrabarti. Dynamic personalized pagerank in entity-relation graphs. In *WWW*, pages 571–580, 2007. DOI: 10.1145/1242572.1242650 120

Gloria Chatzopoulou, Magdalini Eirinaki, and Neoklis Polyzotis. *Query Recommendations for Interactive Database Exploration*, pages 3–18. Springer Berlin Heidelberg, 2009. DOI: 10.1007/978-3-642-02279-1_2 2, 3, 118

Surajit Chaudhuri. Generalization and a framework for query modification. In *ICDE*, pages 138–145, 1990. DOI: 10.1109/icde.1990.113463 12

S. Chen. Six core data wrangling activities ebook, 2015. https://www.trifacta.com/gated-form/6-core-data-wrangling-ebook/ 34

T. Cheng. Toward entity-aware search. Ph.D. thesis, University Of Illinois, Urbana-champaign, 2012. 94

Mitch Cherniack, Michael J. Franklin, and Stanley B. Zdonik. Expressing user profiles for data recharging. *IEEE Personal Communication*, 8(4):32–38, 2001. DOI: 10.1109/98.944001 2

Fernando Chirigati, Harish Doraiswamy, Theodoros Damoulas, and Juliana Freire. Data polygamy: The many-many relationships among urban spatio-temporal data sets. In *SIG-MOD*, pages 1011–1025, 2016. DOI: 10.1145/2882903.2915245 120

Vassilis Christophides, Vasilis Efthymiou, and Kostas Stefanidis. Entity resolution in the web of data. *Synthesis Lectures on the Semantic Web*, 5(3):1–122, 2015. DOI: 10.2200/s00655ed1v01y201507wbe013 29, 94

Edgar F. Codd. A relational model of data for large shared data banks. *Communications of the ACM*, 13(6):377–387, 1970. DOI: 10.1145/357980.358007 11, 12

Soumyarupa De. Newt: An architecture for lineage-based replay and debugging in DISC systems. Ph.D. thesis, UC San Diego, 2012. 11

Colin De la Higuera. *Grammatical Inference: Learning Automata and Grammars*. Cambridge University Press, 2010. DOI: 10.1017/CBO9781139194655 54

Roberto De Virgilio, Antonio Maccioni, and Riccardo Torlone. Converting relational to graph databases. In *GRADES Workshop*, page 1, 2013. DOI: 10.1145/2484425.2484426 90

Arthur P. Dempster, Nan M. Laird, and Donald B. Rubin. Maximum likelihood from incomplete data via the EM algorithm. *Journal of the Royal Statistical Society. Series B (Methodological)*, pages 1–38, 1977. 71

Dong Deng, Raul Castro Fernandez, Ziawasch Abedjan, Sibo Wang, Michael Stonebraker, Ahmed K. Elmagarmid, Ihab F. Ilyas, Samuel Madden, Mourad Ouzzani, and Nan Tang. The data civilizer system. In *CIDR*, 2017. 95

D. Deutch and A. Gilad. QPlain: Query by explanation. In *ICDE*, pages 1358–1361, 2016a. DOI: 10.1109/icde.2016.7498344 33

Daniel Deutch and Amir Gilad. Query by provenance. *ArXiv Preprint ArXiv:1602.03819*, 2016b. 33

Gonzalo Diaz, Marcelo Arenas, and Michael Benedikt. SPARQLByE: Querying RDF data by example. *PVLDB*, 9(13):1533–1536, 2016. DOI: 10.14778/3007263.3007302 39, 55, 57

Kyriaki Dimitriadou, Olga Papaemmanouil, and Yanlei Diao. Explore-by-example: An automatic query steering framework for interactive data exploration. In *SIGMOD*, pages 517–528, 2014. DOI: 10.1145/2588555.2610523 34, 110

Kyriaki Dimitriadou, Olga Papaemmanouil, and Yanlei Diao. Aide: An active learning-based approach for interactive data exploration. *TKDE*, 28(11):2842–2856, 2016. DOI: 10.1109/tkde.2016.2599168 24, 34, 110

Hoang T. Dinh, Chonho Lee, Dusit Niyato, and Ping Wang. A survey of mobile cloud computing: Architecture, applications, and approaches. *Wireless Communications and Mobile Computing*, 13(18):1587–1611, 2013. DOI: 10.1002/wcm.1203 121

Josip Djolonga, Andreas Krause, and Volkan Cevher. High-dimensional Gaussian process bandits. In *NIPS*, pages 1025–1033, 2013. 109

Xin Dong, Evgeniy Gabrilovich, Geremy Heitz, Wilko Horn, Ni Lao, Kevin Murphy, Thomas Strohmann, Shaohua Sun, and Wei Zhang. Knowledge vault: A web-scale approach to probabilistic knowledge fusion. In *KDD*, pages 601–610, 2014. DOI: 10.1145/2623330.2623623 91

John Duchi, Elad Hazan, and Yoram Singer. Adaptive subgradient methods for online learning and stochastic optimization. *JMLR*, 12(Jul):2121–2159, 2011. 102

Khalid El-Arini and Carlos Guestrin. Beyond keyword search: Discovering relevant scientific literature. In *KDD*, pages 439–447, 2011. DOI: 10.1145/2020408.2020479 67, 74, 75, 86

Ahmed El-Roby, Khaled Ammar, Ashraf Aboulnaga, and Jimmy Lin. Sapphire: Querying RDF data made simple. *PVLDB*, 9(13):1481–1484, 2016. DOI: 10.14778/3007263.3007289 121

Martin Ester, Hans-Peter Kriegel, Jörg Sander, and Xiaowei Xu. A density-based algorithm for discovering clusters a density-based algorithm for discovering clusters in large spatial databases with noise. In *KDD*, pages 226–231, AAAI Press, 1996. 73

Ronald Fagin, Laura M. Haas, Mauricio Hernández, Renée J. Miller, Lucian Popa, and Yannis Velegrakis. Clio: Schema mapping creation and data exchange. In *Conceptual Modeling: Foundations and Applications*, pages 198–236, Springer, 2009. DOI: 10.1007/978-3-642-02463-4_12 12

Wenfei Fan, Yinghui Wu, and Jingbo Xu. Functional dependencies for graphs. In *SIGMOD*, pages 1843–1857, 2016. DOI: 10.1145/2882903.2915232 90

Brian Gallagher. Matching structure and semantics: A survey on graph-based pattern matching. *AAAI FS*, 6:45–53, 2006. 61

Mario Arias Gallego, Javier D. Fernández, Miguel A. Martínez-Prieto, and Pablo de la Fuente. An empirical study of real-world SPARQL queries. In *USEWOD Workshop-WWW*, 2011. 55

Venkatesh Ganti and Anish Das Sarma. Data cleaning: A practical perspective. *Synthesis Lectures on Data Management*, 5(3):1–85, 2013. DOI: 10.2200/s00523ed1v01y201307dtm036 28

Hector Garcia-Molina. *Database Systems: The Complete Book*. Pearson Education India, 2008. 14

Claire Gardent, Anastasia Shimorina, Shashi Narayan, and Laura Perez-Beltrachini. The WebNLG challenge: Generating text from RDF data. In *INLG*, pages 124–133, 2017. DOI: 10.18653/v1/w17-3518 91

Marta Garnelo, Dan Rosenbaum, Christopher Maddison, Tiago Ramalho, David Saxton, Murray Shanahan, Yee Whye Teh, Danilo Jimenez Rezende, and S. M. Ali Eslami. Conditional neural processes. In *ICML*, pages 1690–1699, 2018. http://proceedings.mlr.press/v80/garnelo18a.html 108

Roman Garnett, Yamuna Krishnamurthy, Xuehan Xiong, Jeff Schneider, and Richard Mann. Bayesian optimal active search and surveying. In *ICML*, pages 843–850, 2012. 109

Irene Garrigós, Jesús Pardillo, Jose-Norberto Mazón, and Juan Trujillo. A conceptual modeling approach for OLAP personalization. In Alberto H. F. Laender, Silvana Castano, Umeshwar Dayal, Fabio Casati, and José Palazzo M. de Oliveira, Eds., *ER*, pages 401–414, Springer Berlin Heidelberg, 2009. DOI: 10.1007/978-3-642-04840-1_30 120

Aristides Gionis, Michael Mathioudakis, and Antti Ukkonen. Bump hunting in the dark: Local discrepancy maximization on graphs. In *ICDE*, pages 1155–1166, 2015. DOI: 10.1109/icde.2015.7113364 39, 42, 46, 65, 93

Aristides Gionis, Michael Mathioudakis, and Antti Ukkonen. Bump hunting in the dark: Local discrepancy maximization on graphs. *TKDE*, 29(3):529–542, 2017. DOI: 10.1109/icde.2015.7113364 39, 42, 46, 93

Wael H. Gomaa and Aly A. Fahmy. A survey of text similarity approaches. *International Journal of Computer Applications*, 68(13), 2013. DOI: 10.5120/11638-7118 23

Joseph Gonzalez and Sue Ann Hong. Linear-time inverse covariance matrix estimation in Gaussian processes. *Technical Report*, Computer Science Department, Carnegie Mellon University, 2008. 108

Marco Gori and Augusto Pucci. Research paper recommender systems: A random-walk based approach. In *WI*, pages 778–781, 2006. DOI: 10.1109/wi.2006.149 76

Georg Gottlob and Pierre Senellart. Schema mapping discovery from data instances. *JACM*, 57(2):6, 2010. DOI: 10.1145/1667053.1667055 26, 27, 35

Todd J. Green. Containment of conjunctive queries on annotated relations. *Theory of Computing Systems*, 49(2):429–459, 2011. DOI: 10.1007/s00224-011-9327-6 33

Jiafeng Guo, Gu Xu, Xueqi Cheng, and Hang Li. Named entity recognition in query. In *SIGIR*, 2009. DOI: 10.1145/1571941.1571989 78, 94

Daniel Halperin, Victor Teixeira de Almeida, Lee Lee Choo, Shumo Chu, Paraschos Koutris, Dominik Moritz, Jennifer Ortiz, Vaspol Ruamviboonsuk, Jingjing Wang, Andrew Whitaker, et al. Demonstration of the myria big data management service. In *SIGMOD*, pages 881–884, 2014. DOI: 10.1145/2588555.2594530 120

Jialong Han, Kai Zheng, Aixin Sun, Shuo Shang, and Ji-Rong Wen. Discovering neighborhood pattern queries by sample answers in knowledge base. In *ICDE*, pages 1014–1025, 2016. DOI: 10.1109/icde.2016.7498309 51

Maeda F. Hanafi, Azza Abouzied, Laura Chiticariu, and Yunyao Li. SEER: Auto-generating information extraction rules from user-specified examples. In *SIGCHI*, pages 6672–6682, 2017a. DOI: 10.1145/3025453.3025540 67, 81, 87

Maeda F. Hanafi, Azza Abouzied, Laura Chiticariu, and Yunyao Li. Synthesizing extraction rules from user examples with seer. In *SIGMOD*, pages 1687–1690, 2017b. DOI: 10.1145/3035918.3056443 67, 82

Jian He, Enzo Veltri, Donatello Santoro, Guoliang Li, Giansalvatore Mecca, Paolo Papotti, and Nan Tang. Interactive and deterministic data cleaning. In *SIGMOD*, pages 893–907, 2016. DOI: 10.1145/2882903.2915242 30, 32

Joseph M. Hellerstein, Peter J. Haas, and Helen J. Wang. Online aggregation. In *SIGMOD*, pages 171–182, ACM, 1997. DOI: 10.1145/253260.253291 2

Daniel Hernández-Lobato and José Miguel Hernández-Lobato. Scalable Gaussian process classification via expectation propagation. In *AISTATS*, pages 168–176, 2016. 111

Melanie Herschel, Ralf Diestelkämper, and Houssem Ben Lahmar. A survey on provenance: What for? What form? What from? *VLDB Journal*, 26(6):881–906, 2017. DOI: 10.1007/s00778-017-0486-1 11, 33

Steven CH Hoi, Doyen Sahoo, Jing Lu, and Peilin Zhao. Online learning: A comprehensive survey. *ArXiv Preprint ArXiv:1802.02871*, 2018. 100

X. Hu, X. Zhang, C. Lu, E. K. Park, and X. Zhou. Exploiting Wikipedia as external knowledge for document clustering. In *KDD*, 2009. DOI: 10.1145/1557019.1557066 93, 94

Frank K. Hwang, Dana S. Richards, and Pawel Winter. *The Steiner Tree Problem*, vol. 53, Elsevier, 1992. DOI: 10.1002/net.3230220105 45

Stratos Idreos, Martin L. Kersten, Stefan Manegold, et al. Database cracking. In *CIDR*, vol. 7, pages 68–78, 2007. DOI: 10.1145/2619228.2619232 1, 12, 116

Stratos Idreos, Olga Papaemmanouil, and Surajit Chaudhuri. Overview of data exploration techniques. In *SIGMOD*, pages 277–281, 2015. DOI: 10.1145/2723372.2731084 1, 6, 12, 34, 115

Stratos Idreos, Konstantinos Zoumpatianos, Brian Hentschel, Michael S. Kester, and Demi Guo. The data calculator: Data structure design and cost synthesis from first principles, and learned cost models. In *SIGMOD*, 2018. DOI: 10.1145/3183713.3199671 116

Yoshiharu Ishikawa, Ravishankar Subramanya, and Christos Faloutsos. Mindreader: Querying databases through multiple examples. In *VLDB*, 1998. 99, 102

Nandish Jayaram, Mahesh Gupta, Arijit Khan, Chengkai Li, Xifeng Yan, and Ramez Elmasri. GQBE: Querying knowledge graphs by example entity tuples. *ICDE*, pages 1250–1253, 2014. DOI: 10.1109/icde.2016.7498391 66

Nandish Jayaram, Arijit Khan, Chengkai Li, Xifeng Yan, and Ramez Elmasri. Querying knowledge graphs by example entity tuples. *TKDE*, 27(10):2797–2811, 2015. DOI: 10.1109/icde.2016.7498391 39, 58, 59, 64

Glen Jeh and Jennifer Widom. Simrank: A measure of structural-context similarity. In *KDD*, pages 538–543, 2002. DOI: 10.1145/775107.775126 94

Glen Jeh and Jennifer Widom. Scaling personalized web search. In *WWW*, 2003. DOI: 10.1145/775152.775191 41, 63, 94, 120

Haofeng Jia and Erik Saule. An analysis of citation recommender systems: Beyond the obvious. In *ASONAM*, pages 216–223, 2017. DOI: 10.1145/3110025.3110150 67, 76, 86

Lilong Jiang and Arnab Nandi. Snaptoquery: Providing interactive feedback during exploratory query specification. *PVLDB*, 8(11):1250–1261, 2015. DOI: 10.14778/2809974.2809986 121

Kirthevasan Kandasamy, Gautam Dasarathy, Junier B. Oliva, Jeff Schneider, and Barnabás Póczos. Gaussian process bandit optimisation with multi-fidelity evaluations. In *NIPS*, pages 992–1000, 2016. 111

Mehdi Kargar and Aijun An. Keyword search in graphs: Finding r-cliques. *PVLDB*, 4(10):681–692, 2011. DOI: 10.14778/2021017.2021025 94

Richard M. Karp. Reducibility among combinatorial problems. In *Complexity of Computer Computations*, pages 85–103, Springer, 1972. DOI: 10.1007/978-1-4684-2001-2_9 22

Manos Karpathiotakis, Ioannis Alagiannis, and Anastasia Ailamaki. Fast queries over heterogeneous data through engine customization. *PVLDB*, 9(12):972–983, 2016. DOI: 10.14778/2994509.2994516 120

Martin L. Kersten, Stratos Idreos, Stefan Manegold, and Erietta Liarou. The researcher's guide to the data deluge: Querying a scientific database in just a few seconds. *PVLDB*, 4(12):1474–1477, 2011. 2, 3

Arijit Khan, Yinghui Wu, Charu C. Aggarwal, and Xifeng Yan. Nema: Fast graph search with label similarity. In *PVLDB*, vol. 6, pages 181–192, 2013. DOI: 10.14778/2535569.2448952 65, 94

Nodira Khoussainova, Magdalena Balazinska, Wolfgang Gatterbauer, YongChul Kwon, and Dan Suciu. A case for A collaborative query management system. In *CIDR*, 2009. 2

Albert Kim, Liqi Xu, Tarique Siddiqui, Silu Huang, Samuel Madden, and Aditya Parameswaran. Optimally leveraging density and locality for exploratory browsing and sampling. In *HILDA Workshop*, pages 7:1–7:7, ACM, 2018. DOI: 10.1145/3209900.3209903 116

Isabel M. Kloumann and Jon M. Kleinberg. Community membership identification from small seed sets. In *KDD*, pages 1366–1375, 2014. DOI: 10.1145/2623330.2623621 39, 41, 43, 65, 94

André Kohn, Viktor Leis, and Thomas Neumann. Adaptive execution of compiled queries. In *ICDE*, 2018. DOI: 10.1109/icde.2018.00027 116

Andreas Kokkalis, Panagiotis Vagenas, Alexandros Zervakis, Alkis Simitsis, Georgia Koutrika, and Yannis Ioannidis. Logos: A system for translating queries into narratives. In *SIGMOD*, pages 673–676, 2012. DOI: 10.1145/2213836.2213929 90

Tim Kraska, Alex Beutel, Ed H. Chi, Jeffrey Dean, and Neoklis Polyzotis. The case for learned index structures. In *SIGMOD*, pages 489–504, 2018. DOI: 10.1145/3183713.3196909 111

Rajasekar Krishnamurthy, Yunyao Li, Sriram Raghavan, Frederick Reiss, Shivakumar Vaithyanathan, and Huaiyu Zhu. Systemt: A system for declarative information extraction. *SIGMOD Record*, 37(4):7–13, 2009. DOI: 10.1145/1519103.1519105 81

Brian Kulis, et al. Metric learning: A survey. *Foundations and Trends® in Machine Learning*, 5(4):287–364, 2013. DOI: 10.1561/2200000019 94

Jure Leskovec, Anand Rajaraman, and Jeffrey David Ullman. *Mining of Massive Datasets*. Cambridge University Press, 2014. DOI: 10.1017/cbo9781139924801 70

Fei Li and H. V. Jagadish. Understanding natural language queries over relational databases. *SIGMOD Record*, 45(1):6–13, 2016. DOI: 10.1145/2949741.2949744 121

Hao Li, Chee-Yong Chan, and David Maier. Query from examples: An iterative, data-driven approach to query construction. *PVLDB*, 8(13):2158–2169, 2015a. DOI: 10.14778/2831360.2831369 14, 17, 19

Lihong Li, Wei Chu, John Langford, and Robert E. Schapire. A contextual-bandit approach to personalized news article recommendation. In *WWW*, pages 661–670, 2010. DOI: 10.1145/1772690.1772758 106

Xiaoli Li and Bing Liu. Learning to classify texts using positive and unlabeled data. In *IJCAI*, volume 3, pages 587–592, 2003. 70

Yunyao Li, Elmer Kim, Marc A. Touchette, Ramiya Venkatachalam, and Hao Wang. Vinery: A visual IDE for information extraction. *PVLDB*, 8(12):1948–1951, 2015b. DOI: 10.14778/2824032.2824108 81

Thomas Lin, Oren Etzioni, et al. Learning to classify texts using positive and unlabeled data. In *AKBC-WEKEX Workshop*, pages 84–88, 2012. 91, 94

Matteo Lissandrini, Davide Mottin, Themis Palpanas, and Yannis Velegrakis. X2q: Your personal example-based graph explorer. In *PVLDB*, pages 901–904, ACM, 2018a. DOI: 10.14778/3229863.3236251 121

Matteo Lissandrini, Davide Mottin, Themis Palpanas, and Yannis Velegrakis. Multi-example search in rich information graphs. In *ICDE*, 2018b. DOI: 10.1109/icde.2018.00078 63, 64, 66

Bing Liu, Wee Sun Lee, Philip S. Yu, and Xiaoli Li. Partially supervised classification of text documents. In *ICML*, vol. 2, pages 387–394, 2002. 70, 86, 93

Bing Liu, Yang Dai, Xiaoli Li, Wee Sun Lee, and Philip S. Yu. Building text classifiers using positive and unlabeled examples. In *ICDM*, pages 179–186, 2003. DOI: 10.1109/icdm.2003.1250918 67, 69, 70, 71

Yuyu Luo, Xuedi Qin, Nan Tang, and Guoliang Li. Deepeye: Towards automatic data visualization. In *ICDE*, 2018. DOI: 10.1109/icde.2018.00019 117

Shuai Ma, Yang Cao, Wenfei Fan, Jinpeng Huai, and Tianyu Wo. Strong simulation: Capturing topology in graph pattern matching. *TODS*, 39(1):4, 2014. DOI: 10.1145/2528937 60, 61

Yifei Ma, Roman Garnett, and Jeff Schneider. σ-optimality for active learning on Gaussian random fields. In *NIPS*, pages 2751–2759, 2013. 110

Yifei Ma, Tzu-Kuo Huang, and Jeff G. Schneider. Active search and bandits on graphs using sigma-optimality. In *UAI*, pages 542–551, 2015. 99, 109

Andrew McCallum, Kamal Nigam, et al. A comparison of event models for naive Bayes text classification. In *AAAI Workshop on Learning for Text Categorization*, vol. 752, pages 41–48, 1998. 70

Sean M. McNee, Istvan Albert, Dan Cosley, Prateep Gopalkrishnan, Shyong K. Lam, Al Ma-munur Rashid, Joseph A. Konstan, and John Riedl. On the recommending of citations for research papers. In *CSCW*, pages 116–125, 2002. DOI: 10.1145/587095.587096 76

Stephan Mennicke, Jan-Christoph Kalo, and Wolf-Tilo Balke. Querying graph databases: What do graph patterns mean? In *ER*, pages 134–148, 2017. DOI: 10.1007/978-3-319-69904-2_11 61

Steffen Metzger, Ralf Schenkel, and Marcin Sydow. QBEES: Query by entity examples. In *CIKM*, pages 1829–1832, 2013. DOI: 10.1145/2505515.2507873 39, 49, 50, 58, 66

Chaitanya Mishra and Nick Koudas. Interactive query refinement. In *EDBT*, 2009. DOI: 10.1145/1516360.1516459 24

Davide Mottin, Alice Marascu, Senjuti Basu Roy, Gautam Das, Themis Palpanas, and Yannis Velegrakis. A probabilistic optimization framework for the empty-answer problem. *PVLDB*, 6(14):1762–1773, 2013. DOI: 10.14778/2556549.2556560 12, 24

Davide Mottin, Matteo Lissandrini, Yannis Velegrakis, and Themis Palpanas. Exemplar queries: Give me an example of what you need. *PVLDB*, 7(5):365–376, 2014. DOI: 10.14778/2732269.2732273 60, 61, 63

Davide Mottin, Matteo Lissandrini, Yannis Velegrakis, and Themis Palpanas. Exemplar queries: A new way of searching. *VLDB Journal*, pages 1–25, 2016. 39, 60, 61, 63, 66, 93, 145

Fabricio Murai, Diogo Rennó, Bruno Ribeiro, Gisele L. Pappa, Don Towsley, and Krista Gile. Selective harvesting over networks. *ArXiv Preprint ArXiv:1703.05082*, 2017. DOI: 10.1007/s10618-017-0523-0 99

Keerthiram Murugesan and Jaime Carbonell. Active learning from peers. In *NIPS*, pages 7011–7020, 2017. 111

Vivi Nastase, Preslav Nakov, Diarmuid O. Seaghdha, and Stan Szpakowicz. Semantic relations between nominals. *Synthesis lectures on human language technologies*, 6(1):1–119, 2013. DOI: 10.2200/s00489ed1v01y201303hlt019 86

Felix Naumann. Data profiling revisited. *ACM SIGMOD Record*, 42(4):40–49, 2014. DOI: 10.1145/2590989.2590995 34

Tam T. Nguyen, Kuiyu Chang, and Siu Cheung Hui. Two-view online learning. In *PAKDD*, pages 74–85, 2012. DOI: 10.1007/978-3-642-30217-6_7 103

Michael O'Donnell, Alistair Knott, Jon Oberlander, and Chris Mellish. Optimising text quality in generation from relational databases. In *ACL*, pages 133–140, 2000.

Kenton O'hara, Richard Harper, Helena Mentis, Abigail Sellen, and Alex Taylor. On the naturalness of touchless: Putting the "interaction" back into NUI. *TOCHI*, 20(1):5, 2013. DOI: 10.1145/2442106.2442111 121

Ognjen Orel, Slaven Zakošek, and Mirta Baranovič. Property oriented relational-to-graph database conversion. *automatika*, 57(3):836–845, 2016.

Laurel Orr, Magdalena Balazinska, and Dan Suciu. Probabilistic database summarization for interactive data exploration. *PVLDB*, 10(10):1154–1165, 2017. DOI: 10.14778/3115404.3115419 118

Lawrence Page, Sergey Brin, Rajeev Motwani, and Terry Winograd. The pagerank citation ranking: Bringing order to the Web. TR 1999–66, Stanford InfoLab, Nov. 94

Kiril Panev and Sebastian Michel. Reverse engineering top-k database queries with paleo. In *EDBT*, pages 113–124, 2016. 20, 23

George Papadakis and Themis Palpanas. Web-scale, schema-agnostic, end-to-end entity resolution (tutorial). In *WWW*, 2018. 29, 94

George Papadakis, George Alexiou, George Papastefanatos, and Georgia Koutrika. Schema-agnostic vs. schema-based configurations for blocking methods on homogeneous data. *PVLDB*, 9(4):312–323, 2015. DOI: 10.14778/2856318.2856326 29

George Papadakis, Jonathan Svirsky, Avigdor Gal, and Themis Palpanas. Comparative analysis of approximate blocking techniques for entity resolution. *PVLDB*, 9(9):684–695, 2016. DOI: 10.14778/2947618.2947624 29

George Papadakis, Leonidas Tsekouras, Emmanouil Thanos, George Giannakopoulos, Themis Palpanas, and Manolis Koubarakis. The return of Jedai: End-to-end entity resolution for structured and semi-structured data. *PVLDB*, 11(12):1950–1953, 2018. DOI: 10.14778/3229863.3236232 29

Christos H. Papadimitriou. *Computational Complexity*. John Wiley & Sons Ltd., 2003. 31

Dimitra Papadimitriou, Georgia Koutrika, Yannis Velegrakis, and John Mylopoulos. Finding related forum posts through content similarity over intention-based segmentation. *TKDE*, 29(9):1860–1873, 2017. DOI: 10.1109/icde.2018.00260 67, 72, 73, 86

Olga Papaemmanouil, Yanlei Diao, Kyriaki Dimitriadou, and Liping Peng. Interactive data exploration via machine learning models. *IEEE Data Engineering Bulletin*, 39(4):38–49, 2016. 119

Aditya Parameswaran, Neoklis Polyzotis, and Hector Garcia-Molina. SeeDB: Visualizing database queries efficiently. *PVLDB*, 7(4):325–328, December 2013. DOI: 10.14778/2732240.2732250 2

David Park. *Concurrency and Automata on Infinite Sequences.* Springer, 1981. DOI: 10.1007/bfb0017309 61

Jorge Pérez, Marcelo Arenas, and Claudio Gutierrez. Semantics and complexity of SPARQL. *TODS*, 34(3):16, 2009. DOI: 10.1145/1567274.1567278 55

Laura Perez-Beltrachini, Rania Sayed, and Claire Gardent. Building RDF content for data-to-text generation. In *COLING*, 2016. 91

Bryan Perozzi, Leman Akoglu, Patricia Iglesias Sánchez, and Emmanuel Müller. Focused clustering and outlier detection in large attributed graphs. In *KDD*, pages 1346–1355, 2014. DOI: 10.1145/2623330.2623682 39, 47, 48, 51, 65, 93, 120

Robert Pienta, James Abello, Minsuk Kahng, and Duen Horng Chau. Scalable graph exploration and visualization: Sensemaking challenges and opportunities. In *BigComp*, pages 271–278, 2015. DOI: 10.1109/35021bigcomp.2015.7072812 117

Robert Pienta, Fred Hohman, Acar Tamersoy, Alex Endert, Shamkant Navathe, Hanghang Tong, and Duen Horng Chau. Visual graph query construction and refinement. In *SIGMOD*, pages 1587–1590, 2017. DOI: 10.1145/3035918.3056418 117

Lucian Popa, Yannis Velegrakis, Mauricio A. Hernández, Renée J. Miller, and Ronald Fagin. Translating web data. In *VLDB*, pages 598–609, 2002. DOI: 10.1016/b978-155860869-6/50059-7 25

Giulia Preti, Matteo Lissandrini, Davide Mottin, and Yannis Velegrakis. Beyond frequencies: Graph pattern mining in multi-weighted graphs. In *EDBT*, pages 169–180, 2018. 120

Fotis Psallidas, Bolin Ding, Kaushik Chakrabarti, and Surajit Chaudhuri. S4: Top-k spreadsheet-style search for query discovery. In *SIGMOD*, pages 2001–2016, 2015. DOI: 10.1145/2723372.2749452 20, 22, 23

Bhavani Raskutti, Herman L. Ferrá, and Adam Kowalczyk. Using unlabelled data for text classification through addition of cluster parameters. In *ICML*, pages 514–521, 2002. 70

Carl Edward Rasmussen. Gaussian processes in machine learning. In *Advanced Lectures on Machine Learning*, pages 63–71, Springer, 2004. DOI: 10.1007/978-3-540-28650-9_4 107

Alan Ritter, Sam Clark, Mausam, and Oren Etzioni. Named entity recognition in tweets: An experimental study. In *EMNLP*, ACL, 2011. 78, 87

Alan Ritter, Evan Wright, William Casey, and Tom Mitchell. Weakly supervised extraction of computer security events from twitter. In *WWW*, pages 896–905, 2015. DOI: 10.1145/2736277.2741083 67, 82

Thomas Roelleke. Information retrieval models: Foundations and relationships. *Synthesis Lectures on Information Concepts, Retrieval, and Services*, 5(3):1–163, 2013. DOI: 10.2200/s00494ed1v01y201304icr027 92

Senjuti Basu Roy, Haidong Wang, Ullas Nambiar, Gautam Das, and Mukesh Mohania. DynaCet: Building dynamic faceted search systems over databases. In *ICDE*, pages 1463–1466, 2009. DOI: 10.1109/icde.2009.117 119

Natali Ruchansky, Francesco Bonchi, David García-Soriano, Francesco Gullo, and Nicolas Kourtellis. The minimum Wiener connector problem. In *SIGMOD*, pages 1587–1602, 2015. DOI: 10.1145/2723372.2749449 39, 42, 44, 45, 65

Eldar Sadikov, Jayant Madhavan, Lu Wang, and Alon Halevy. Clustering query refinements by user intent. In *WWW*, pages 841–850, ACM, 2010. DOI: 10.1145/1772690.1772776 2

Jean Scholtz. User-centered evaluation of visual analytics. *Synthesis Lectures on Visualization*, 1(1):1–71, 2017. DOI: 10.2200/s00797ed1v01y201709vis009 117

Thibault Sellam and Martin Kersten. Cluster-driven navigation of the query space. *TKDE*, 28(5):1118–1131, 2016a. DOI: 10.1109/tkde.2016.2515590 33

Thibault Sellam and Martin Kersten. Ziggy: Characterizing query results for data explorers. *PVLDB*, 9(13):1473–1476, 2016b. DOI: 10.14778/3007263.3007287 33, 34

Thibault Sellam, Martin L. Kersten, et al. Meet Charles, big data query advisor. In *CIDR*, vol. 13, page 1, 2013. 118

Burr Settles. Active learning. *Synthesis Lectures on Artificial Intelligence and Machine Learning*, 6(1):1–114, 2012. DOI: 10.2200/s00429ed1v01y201207aim018 104

Wei Shen, Jianyong Wang, and Jiawei Han. Entity linking with a knowledge base: Issues, techniques, and solutions. *TKDE*, 27(2):443–460, 2015. DOI: 10.1109/tkde.2014.2327028 93, 94

Yanyan Shen, Kaushik Chakrabarti, Surajit Chaudhuri, Bolin Ding, and Lev Novik. Discovering queries based on example tuples. In *SIGMOD*, pages 493–504, 2014. DOI: 10.1145/2588555.2593664 20, 21

Jaeho Shin, Sen Wu, Feiran Wang, Christopher De Sa, Ce Zhang, and Christopher Ré. Incremental knowledge base construction using deepdive. *PVLDB*, 8(11):1310–1321, 2015. DOI: 10.14778/2809974.2809991 86

Milad Shokouhi. Learning to personalize query auto-completion. In *SIGIR*, pages 103–112, ACM, 2013. DOI: 10.1145/2484028.2484076 120

Tarique Siddiqui, Albert Kim, John Lee, Karrie Karahalios, and Aditya Parameswaran. Effortless data exploration with zenvisage: An expressive and interactive visual analytics system. *PVLDB*, 10(4):457–468, 2016. DOI: 10.14778/3025111.3025126 117

Manpreet Singh, Karamjit Kaur, et al. Sql2neo: Moving health-care data from rela- tional to graph databases. In *IACC*, pages 721–725, 2015.

Rishabh Singh. Blinkfill: Semi-supervised programming by example for syntactic string transformations. *PVLDB*, 9(10):816–827, 2016. DOI: 10.14778/2977797.2977807 35

Rohit Singh, Venkata Vamsikrishna Meduri, Ahmed Elmagarmid, Samuel Madden, Paolo Papotti, Jorge-Arnulfo Quiané-Ruiz, Armando Solar-Lezama, and Nan Tang. Synthesizing entity matching rules by examples. *PVLDB*, 11(2):189–202, 2017. DOI: 10.14778/3149193.3149199 30, 94

Grzegorz Sobczak, Mateusz Chochół, Ralf Schenkel, and Marcin Sydow. iQbees: Towards interactive semantic entity search based on maximal aspects. In *Foundations of Intelligent Systems*, pages 259–264, Springer, 2015. DOI: 10.1007/978-3-319-25252-0_28 39, 49, 50, 52, 66

Armando Solar-Lezama. The sketching approach to program synthesis. In *APLAS*, pages 4–13, 2009. DOI: 10.1007/978-3-642-10672-9_3 30

Qi Song, Yinghui Wu, and Xin Luna Dong. Mining summaries for knowledge graph search. In *ICDM*, pages 1215–1220, 2016. DOI: 10.1109/icdm.2016.0162 65, 118

Yangqiu Song, Haixun Wang, Zhongyuan Wang, Hongsong Li, and Weizhu Chen. Short text conceptualization using a probabilistic knowledgebase. In *IJCAI*, 2011. 91, 94

Yinglong Song, Huey Eng Chua, Sourav S. Bhowmick, Byron Choi, and Shuigeng Zhou. Boomer: Blending visual formulation and processing of p-homomorphic queries on large networks. In *SIGMOD*, pages 927–942, 2018. DOI: 10.1145/3183713.3196902 117

Niranjan Srinivas, Andreas Krause, Sham Kakade, and Matthias Seeger. Gaussian process optimization in the bandit setting: No regret and experimental design. In *ICML*, pages 1015–1022, 2010. 108, 109

Yu Su, Shengqi Yang, Huan Sun, Mudhakar Srivatsa, Sue Kase, Michelle Vanni, and Xifeng Yan. Exploiting relevance feedback in knowledge graph search. In *KDD*, pages 1135–1144, 2015. DOI: 10.1145/2783258.2783320 99

Fabian M. Suchanek, Gjergji Kasneci, and Gerhard Weikum. Yago: A core of semantic knowledge. In *WWW*, pages 697–706, 2007. DOI: 10.1145/1242572.1242667 91

Bo Tang, Shi Han, Man Lung Yiu, Rui Ding, and Dongmei Zhang. Extracting top-k insights from multi-dimensional data. In *SIGMOD*, pages 1509–1524, 2017. DOI: 10.1145/3035918.3035922 117

Jaime Teevan, Susan T. Dumais, and Eric Horvitz. Personalizing search via automated analysis of interests and activities. In *SIGIR*, pages 449–456, ACM, 2005. DOI: 10.1145/3190580.3190582 120

Balder Ten Cate, Phokion G. Kolaitis, and Wang-Chiew Tan. Schema mappings and data examples. In *EDBT/ICDT*, pages 777–780, 2013. DOI: 10.1145/2452376.2452479 25

Christian Tominski. Interaction for visualization. *Synthesis Lectures on Visualization*, 1(1):1–107, 2015. DOI: 10.2200/s00651ed1v01y201506vis003 117

Hanghang Tong and Christos Faloutsos. Center-piece subgraphs: Problem definition and fast solutions. In *KDD*, pages 404–413, 2006. DOI: 10.1145/1150402.1150448 42, 43

Quoc Trung Tran and Chee-Yong Chan. How to conquer why-not questions. In *SIGMOD*, pages 15–26, 2010. DOI: 10.1145/1807167.1807172 11

Quoc Trung Tran, Chee-Yong Chan, and Srinivasan Parthasarathy. Query by output. In *SIGMOD*, pages 535–548, 2009. DOI: 10.1145/1559845.1559902 14, 15, 19

Quoc Trung Tran, Chee-Yong Chan, and Srinivasan Parthasarathy. Query reverse engineering. *VLDB Journal*, 23(5):721–746, 2014. DOI: 10.1007/s00778-013-0349-3 14

Bayu Distiawan Trisedya, Jianzhong Qi, Rui Zhang, and Wei Wang. GTR-LSTM: A triple encoder for sentence generation from RDF data. In *ACL*, vol. 1, pages 1627–1637, 2018. 91

D. Vallet and P. Castells. Personalized diversification of search results. In *SIGIR*, 2012. DOI: 10.1145/2348283.2348396 120

Vladimir Vapnik. *The Nature of Statistical Learning Theory*. Springer Science and Business Media, 2013. DOI: 10.1007/978-1-4757-3264-1 71

Manasi Vartak, Silu Huang, Tarique Siddiqui, Samuel Madden, and Aditya Parameswaran. Towards visualization recommendation systems. *SIGMOD Record*, 45(4):34–39, 2017. DOI: 10.1145/3092931.3092937 2, 117

Martin J. Wainwright, Erik B. Sudderth, and Alan S. Willsky. Tree-based modeling and estimation of Gaussian processes on graphs with cycles. In *NIPS*, pages 661–667, 2001. DOI: 10.1109/tsp.2004.836539 108

Chi Wang, Kaushik Chakrabarti, Yeye He, Kris Ganjam, Zhimin Chen, and Philip A. Bernstein. Concept expansion using web tables. In *WWW*, pages 1198–1208, 2015. DOI: 10.1145/2736277.2741644 67, 82, 83, 84, 87

Dan Wang and Xing hua Fan. Named entity recognition for short text. *Journal of Computer Applications*, 29:143–145, 2009. DOI: 10.3724/sp.j.1087.2009.00143 78, 94

Quan Wang, Zhendong Mao, Bin Wang, and Li Guo. Knowledge graph embedding: A survey of approaches and applications. *TKDE*, 29(12):2724–2743, 2017. DOI: 10.1109/tkde.2017.2754499 94

Abdul Wasay, Manos Athanassoulis, and Stratos Idreos. Queriosity: Automated data exploration. In *BigData*, 2015. DOI: 10.1109/bigdatacongress.2015.116 7, 115, 117

Abdul Wasay, Xinding Wei, Niv Dayan, and Stratos Idreos. Data canopy: Accelerating exploratory statistical analysis. In *CIKM*, pages 557–572, 2017. DOI: 10.1145/3035918.3064051 116

Cathrin Weiss, Panagiotis Karras, and Abraham Bernstein. Hexastore: Sextuple indexing for semantic web data management. *PVLDB*, 1(1):1008–1019, 2008. DOI: 10.14778/1453856.1453965 91

Yaacov Y. Weiss and Sara Cohen. Reverse engineering SPJ-queries from examples. In *PODS*, pages 151–166, 2017. DOI: 10.1145/3034786.3056112 14, 15, 19, 35

Jeremy West, Dan Ventura, and Sean Warnick. Spring research presentation: A theoretical foundation for inductive transfer. Brigham Young University, College of Physical and Mathematical Sciences, 1, 2007. 32

Ryen W. White and Resa A. Roth. Exploratory search: Beyond the query-response paradigm. *Synthesis Lectures on Information Concepts, Retrieval, and Services*, 1(1):1–98, 2009. DOI: 10.2200/s00174ed1v01y200901icr003 3, 77, 113, 114

Harry Wiener. Structural determination of paraffin boiling points. *Journal of the American Chemical Society*, 69(1):17–20, 1947. DOI: 10.1021/ja01193a005 44

Rudolf Wille. Restructuring lattice theory: An approach based on hierarchies of concepts. In *International Conference on Formal Concept Analysis*, pages 314–339, 2009. DOI: 10.1007/978-3-642-01815-2_23 3, 4

Peter T. Wood. Query languages for graph databases. *SIGMOD Record*, 41(1):50–60, 2012. DOI: 10.1145/2206869.2206879 52

Eugene Wu, Leilani Battle, and Samuel R. Madden. The case for data visualization management systems: Vision paper. *PVLDB*, 7(10):903–906, 2014. DOI: 10.14778/2732951.2732964 2, 7

Miao Xie, Sourav S. Bhowmick, Gao Cong, and Qing Wang. Panda: Toward partial topology-based search on large networks in a single machine. *VLDB Journal*, 26(2):203–228, 2017. DOI: 10.1007/s00778-016-0447-0 64

Eric P. Xing, Michael I. Jordan, Stuart J. Russell, and Andrew Y. Ng. Distance metric learning with application to clustering with side-information. In *NIPS*, pages 521–528, 2003. 48

Konstantinos Xirogiannopoulos and Amol Deshpande. Extracting and analyzing hidden graphs from relational databases. In *SISMOD*, pages 897–912, 2017. DOI: 10.1145/3035918.3035949 90

Konstantinos Xirogiannopoulos, Udayan Khurana, and Amol Deshpande. Graphgen: Exploring interesting graphs in relational data. *PVLDB*, 8(12):2032–2035, 2015. DOI: 10.14778/2824032.2824129 90

Mohamed Yakout, Kris Ganjam, Kaushik Chakrabarti, and Surajit Chaudhuri. Infogather: Entity augmentation and attribute discovery by holistic matching with web tables. In *SIGMOD*, 2012. DOI: 10.1145/2213836.2213848 67, 82, 84, 85, 87

Ling Ling Yan, Renée J. Miller, Laura M. Haas, and Ronald Fagin. Data-driven understanding and refinement of schema mappings. In *SIGMOD*, vol. 30, pages 485–496, 2001. DOI: 10.1145/375663.375729 25

Hwanjo Yu, Jiawei Han, and Kevin Chen-Chuan Chang. PEBL: Positive example based learning for web page classification using SVM. In *KDD*, pages 239–248, 2002. DOI: 10.1145/775082.775083 70

Jeffrey Xu Yu, Lu Qin, and Lijun Chang. *Keyword Search in Databases*, 1st ed., Morgan & Claypool Publishers, 2010. 90
DOI: 10.2200/s00231ed1v01y200912dtm001

Dell Zhang and Wee Sun Lee. Query-by-multiple-examples using support vector machines. *JDIM*, 7(4):202–210, 2009. 67, 71, 86

Meihui Zhang, Hazem Elmeleegy, Cecilia M. Procopiuc, and Divesh Srivastava. Reverse engineering complex join queries. In *SIGMOD*, pages 809–820, 2013. DOI: 10.1145/2463676.2465320 14, 17

Zhu Zhang. Mining relational data from text: From strictly supervised to weakly supervised learning. *Information Systems*, 33(3):300–314, 2008. DOI: 10.1016/j.is.2007.10.002 91

Mingzhu Zhu and Yi-Fang Brook Wu. Search by multiple examples. In *WSDM*, pages 667–672, 2014. DOI: 10.1145/2556195.2556206 67, 71

Mingzhu Zhu, Chao Xu, and Yi-Fang Brook Wu. IFME: Information filtering by multiple examples with under-sampling in a digital library environment. In *JCDL*, pages 107–110, 2013. DOI: 10.1145/2467696.2467736 67, 71, 86

Moshé M. Zloof.   Query by example.   In *AFIPS NCC*, pages 431–438, 1975. DOI: 10.1145/1499799.1499914 4, 56, 58

Kostas Zoumpatianos, Stratos Idreos, and Themis Palpanas. ADS: The adaptive data series index. *VLDB Journal*, 25(6):843–866, 2016. DOI: 10.1007/s00778-016-0442-5 116

Authors' Biographies

MATTEO LISSANDRINI

Matteo Lissandrini is a postdoctoral researcher at Aalborg University. He received his Ph.D. in Computer Science at the University of Trento, Italy, where he was member of the Data and Information Management (dbTrento) research group. He received his M.Sc. in Computer Science from the university of Trento, Italy, and his B.Sc. Computer Science from the University of Verona, Italy. He has also spent time as a visitor at HP Labs, Palo Alto, California, at the Cheriton School of Computer Science at the University of Waterloo, Canada, and at the Laboratory for Foundations of Computer Science (LFCS) at the University of Edinburgh, United Kingdom. His scientific interests include novel query paradigms for large scale data mining and information extraction with a focus on exploratory search on graph data. He published the first paper on Exemplar Query methods for Knowledge Graphs in VLDB and VLDBJ, and presented the application of such methods in SIGMOD 2014 and VLDB 2018.

DAVIDE MOTTIN

Davide Mottin is a faculty member at Aarhus University with expertise in graph mining, exploratory methods, and user interaction. Before he was a postdoctoral researcher at Hasso Plattner Institute, leading the graph mining subgroup in the Knowledge Discovery and Data Mining group. He presented graph exploration tutorials in CIKM 2016, SIGMOD 2017, and KDD 2018. He also presented exploratory techniques in KDD 2015, VLDB 2014, and SIGMOD 2015 and is actively engaged in teaching database, big data analytics, and graph mining for Bachelor and Master courses. He is the proponent of exemplar queries paradigm for exploratory analysis [Mottin et al., 2016]. He received his Ph.D. in 2015 from the University of Trento and his thesis was awarded as "The best of the department in 2015." He has also visited Yahoo! Labs in Barcelona and Microsoft Research Asia in Beijing.

THEMIS PALPANAS

Themis Palpanas is Senior Member of the French University Institute (IUF), and Professor of computer science at the Paris Descartes University (France), where he is the director of diNo, the data management group. He received the B.Sc. from the National Technical University of Athens, Greece, and the M.Sc. and Ph.D. from the University of Toronto, Canada. He has previously held positions at the IBM T.J. Watson Research Center (U.S.), and the University of Trento (Italy). He has also worked for the University of California at Riverside, and visited Microsoft Research (U.S.) and the IBM Almaden Research Center (U.S.). His research interests include problems related to online and offline data management and data analytics, focusing on exploratory search using knowledge graphs, entity resolution on very large and heterogeneous data, and data series similarity search and analytics. He is the author of nine U.S. patents, three of which have been implemented in world-leading commercial data management products. He is the recipient of three Best Paper awards, and the IBM Shared University Research (SUR) Award. He is serving as Editor in Chief for *BDR Journal*, Associate Editor for *PVLDB 2019*, and *TKDE* journal, and Editorial Advisory Board member for *IS* journal. He has also served (among others) as General Chair for VLDB 2013, Associate Editor for PVLDB 2017, and Workshop Chair for EDBT 2016.

YANNIS VELEGRAKIS

Yannis Velegrakis is a faculty member in the Department of Information Engineering and Computer Science of the University of Trento, director of the Data Management Group, head of the Data and Knowledge Management Research Program, and coordinator of its EIT Digital Master. His research area of expertise includes Big Data Management, Analytics and Exploration, Knowledge Discovery, Highly Heterogeneous Information Integration, User-centred Querying, Personalisation, Recommendation, Graph Management, and Data Quality. Before joining the University of Trento, he was a researcher at the AT&T Research Labs. He has spent time as a visitor at the IBM Almaden Research Centre (U.S.), the IBM Toronto Lab (Canada), the University of California, Santa-Cruz (U.S.), the University of Paris-Saclay (France), and the Huawei Research Center (Germany). His work has also been recognized through a Marie Curie and a Université Paris-Saclay Jean D'Alembert fellowship. He has been an active member of the database community. He has served as the General Chair for VLDB'13, PC Area chair for ICDE'18, and PC chair in a number of other conferences/workshops.

Printed in the United States
by Baker & Taylor Publisher Services